# I CAN DEPEND ON ME

Valarie,
Thanks so much for your support. all the best of health, love & success!
Shar...

# I CAN *DEPEND* ON ME

Sharron Jamison

Library of Congress Control Number: 2012918275

| ISBN: | Hardcover | 978-1-4797-2593-9 |
| --- | --- | --- |
| | Softcover | 978-1-4797-2592-2 |
| | Ebook | 978-1-4797-2594-6 |



This book was printed in the United States of America.

**To order additional copies of this book, contact:**
Xlibris Corporation
1-888-795-4274
www.Xlibris.com
Orders@Xlibris.com
120782

# CONTENTS

# FOREWORD

IT IS A rare and blessed occasion to find yourself in the company of women who impact your life by their mere presence. These women live life out loud and unapologetically. I have had the good fortune of encountering several of these living angels throughout my life. SharRon Jamison is certainly among these women for me. Her energy is so dynamic that it could quite easily energize the room without intending to do so. However her compassion and God-centered empathy, instead, makes room for everyone's divinity. I am in constant awe of her ability to affirm others in her space. She has a heart as expansive as her presence. Her book is a gift. It is the kind of spiritual endowment that explodes with raw, vulnerable truth in her first book, *I Can Depend on Me*. SharRon generously serves up pieces of her soul with stories of surviving racism and struggles of personal growth. She does so for each of us to see our own story in hers. You will be warmed by it. You will be uplifted by it.

*I Can Depend on Me* is a written feast of passion, honesty, and triumph over painful experiences. If you open your heart, it will be an opportunity to feed your soul and nourish your spirit beyond adversity. Some of the stories will make you giggle with childish reminiscence, and yet other stories will evoke anger for the injustice and hurt they ignite. Whatever your experience, I invite you to expand your emotional palate and partake of this spiritual journey with SharRon Jamison in *I Can Depend on Me!*

Imani Evans, MA, BA
Empowerment Coach/Activist/Author
Women Healing Women, Inc.

# PREFACE

I HAVE FACED many battles in my life, but the hardest and most valiant battle was against depression. For more than thirty years, I struggled with the pervasive, energy-draining feeling of dread and gloom. I constantly suffered from a feeling of emotional heaviness and physical lethargy. The perpetual feelings of despair engulfed me, and I constantly felt as if happiness and joy were unattainable. I did not understand why I was feeling so sad. I tried to find answers, but in most African American communities in early 1970s, depression was not discussed. I never even heard of the term depression until I completed college. All I knew was that telling people that I felt downcast and hopeless was met with admonitions to "stay strong," "pray about it," or "if God brought you to it, God will bring you through it." That was it. No good advice, no additional counseling, no shared wisdom was offered. I was instructed to pray. What many did not realize was that I was so dejected that remembering how to pray or initiating prayer by myself took too much effort. All my energy was used to survive and perform in school, serve in my father's church, and exist in a family that was always in transition. What I later learned in life was that my experience was similar to the experiences of others who struggled with depression and feelings of discouragement. To better understand my depression, I dissected my life. I identified the roots of my pain, pinpointed the origin of my loneliness, and uncovered the causes of my helplessness. I used all of my resolve to devise a road to my recovery and healing.

This book is the result of reviewing my journals, working with therapists, sharing with my friends and my sister circles. My depression has many etiologies, but my most prominent causes centered around unresolved pain and undisclosed fear suffered in childhood. The hurtful and toxic emotions produced a malignant wound that threatened the health of my spirit. I thankfully had teachers, guides, and friends who helped in my healing journey. Dealing with depression was and still is difficult. It is an illness that many people do not understand, cannot see, or will not accept. But I now know that the experiences in my life that have taught me the most about me are the experiences that trapped me in guilt and shame. But I am now free of the shame and stigma of depression. And I learned one important lesson during my recovery—"I can depend on me, just God and me."

## CHAPTER 1

# Welcome to the Real World

*SEPTEMBER 7.* I thought the day would never arrive. September 7 was the day that I had waited and prayed for all summer to come, and it was finally here. I was extremely excited, so excited that I slept little the night before. I was happy about wearing my new school clothes, and taking my Fat Albert lunch box to school. My Fat Albert lunchbox was special to me, and my mother had looked everywhere for it. It was hard to find because every Black child had to have a Fat Albert lunchbox. In the early 1970s, Fat Albert was as top-rated Saturday cartoon and one of the only Black shows on TV. But honestly, I really didn't care much about Fat Albert. I just wanted a lunch box with Black faces on it, and Fat Albert was it—the black-face lunchbox.

During the summer in University City, Missouri, I had practically tortured my mother and big sister with questions about school. My sister told me about recess, coloring time, nap time, and library time. My mother had convinced me that only big girls went to school and, boy, did I feel honored to finally be a "big girl." That morning when I was getting dressed and feeling a little nervous, my mother again reminded that "only big girls go to school and now you are a big girl." It is amazing how words can lose their comforting effect in the face of fear. Just a few weeks prior, I believed that I was a big girl ready to attend school. But today, September 7, fear gripped me; and I felt awkward and unsettled.

When I arrived at school, I felt out of place. Nobody looked like me. Everybody had long brown or blonde hair with bows and ribbons. Nobody had skin that looked like mine; they were white. I had seen White people before on TV and in stores, but I had never been around them. I had mostly lived and interacted with Blacks. For some reason, I knew that Blacks and Whites did not get along too well. I had never seen any fights or anything, but I did notice that my parents acted and behaved differently when Whites were around. They talked differently, especially my mother.

My mother sounded as if she was attempting to talk through her nose, and she seemed to over-pronounce words. It was a voice we Black kids termed as the "White people voice." We didn't judge it; we just accepted that Blacks had to be different when White adults were around. Anyway, I never talked to grown White people without my parent's permission and presence, and I felt a little unsure if I should talk to White children without asking my parents' permission too. Not knowing what to do, I became anxious and panicked.

When I walked into the classroom, the room looked gigantic. For some reason, I thought that the classroom would be the same size as my Sunday school room at church, but it was twice as large. As I stepped into the room, I proceeded to take it all in. The room was aptly decorated for learning with oversized letters, exciting shapes and all the primary colors adorning the walls. I saw buckets of crayons, boxes of colored pencils, a carton filled with small containers of paste, and a place reserved for lunchboxes. I noticed pictures of white kids participating in different activities, but no Black kids. I was not too concerned because I was accustomed to not seeing representations of Blacks in catalogs, in books, in stores, or on TV. So not having any pictures of Blacks did not initially alarm me; it was familiar. Suffice it to say that entering into my kindergarten classroom was overwhelming, disconcerting, and exhilarating all at the same time.

I also observed the teacher, and she appeared to be nice. She spoke to all of the White kids and their parents. She did not say anything to me and Momma, but that did not concern me either. Most Whites never acknowledged me and my mother when we visited stores, went to the park, went to a Laundromat, or went to Burger Chef. So being ignored felt somewhat normal. I had been socialized and in many ways reared to accept being a second-class citizen. And as a result, I did not really expect to receive the same treatment as my White classmates. Nobody ever fully explained why I would be treated differently, but nobody had to either. It was an unspoken truth. I would receive *less*—less attention, less time, less snacks, less consideration, and less fun. Receiving less was somehow acceptable to me, and it was the most that I hoped for; and unconsciously, it was what I expected. I predicted, assumed, and anticipated less, less of everything.

After the morning bell rang, the teacher called roll. I could not wait until she said my name because I would finally have an opportunity to use my nasal voice, my White people voice, like my mother used. The teacher called, "Sharon Jamison." I proudly corrected her; and in my most nasal sounding voice, I said, "SharRon." I was proud of my name because grown-ups said that my name was unique. I did not know what unique meant, but it sounded important. And since adults said that my name sounded important, I felt important. After I corrected my teacher, she said, "I'll call you Sharon." Almost in tears, I said, "No, my name is SharRon." I wanted to protest but I did not know how. I didn't know what else to say to object to my name being mispronounced. I felt relieved that she went on to the next person's name because the class and some of the parents were staring at me. I did like getting attention from people, but I felt uncomfortable having a room full of White people staring at me. It was unsettling, and I felt frightened and overly anxious.

Before my mother returned home from work, I debated as to whether I should tell her that Ms. Applegate called me Sharon and not SharRon. I was angry and felt slighted that she called me Sharon after I pronounced my name correctly for her. I was also hurt that the other kids were called by their appropriate names and I was not. To make sure my mother realized how I upset I was, I planned to cry as soon as she opened the front door. I had to ensure that she became more upset at Ms. Applegate for mispronouncing my name rather than at me for correcting Ms. Applegate, a White woman, in public. I was taught against correcting adults, but I understood that correcting a White woman was regarded as especially disrespectful. I was not taught that White people should be held in higher regard, I just observed it. So I was acutely aware of the unspoken message and abided by the unspoken yet socially mandated directive.

As I heard her in the driveway, I immediately started my crying act. I explained that Ms. Applegate called me Sharon, and I told her that my name was SharRon. My mother smiled and told me that she was proud of me for "helping" Ms. Applegate pronounce my name correctly. My mother promised to go to school with me the next day to make sure the teacher pronounced my name correctly. I felt relieved because I was uneasy correcting a White woman in public, and I wasn't sure if I would be brave enough to correct her again.

The next morning, I got up bright and early, ready to go to school. Even though I was still upset, I felt good that Momma was going to talk to my teacher about my name. I hurried to dress, put my lunch in my Fat Albert lunchbox, and off we went. As I walked the hallways holding Momma's hand, I realized that people were staring at us. I did not understand why then, but my mother later explained that some White people were upset that Black people were being "bussed." I did not understand what being "bussed" meant and I did not care. I just wanted to go to school, carry my Fat Albert lunchbox, and be called by my name, my unique name.

When we arrived at my classroom, Ms. Applegate looked at us, but then ignored us. It was as if we were invisible, so Momma walked over to her and said, "Hi, I am Mrs. Jamison, SharRon's mother." Ms. Applegate frowned and said, "What's your first name?" My mother replied firmly and very intentionally in her White people voice, "My name is Mrs. Jamison." I was confused by my mother's insistence on being called by her last name because she had taught me that grown-ups can call each other by their first names; only children had to say mister or missus. But I sensed that Momma did not want my teacher to call her by her first name. The tension was evident, and I started to sweat. Ms. Applegate turned red and appeared nervous, but my mother did not budge or blink. I just thought that Ms. Applegate was intimidated by Momma because Momma was taller than her. I almost started to ask Ms. Applegate, "Are you scared of my momma?" but I didn't. Something in my mother's eyes and in her demeanor told me to remain silent. I felt as if Momma and Ms. Applegate were having a standoff.

After what appeared to be three days, my mother pleasantly explained that my name was SharRon, and that I was very proud of my name. My mother said, "I would appreciate you calling her by her name too." I was proud of my mother especially because I knew that she was a little anxious confronting my teacher. Her discomfort was obvious to me, but her resolve to protect me was greater than her fear. I could tell that she had rehearsed the exchange so that she would be taken seriously. Her eye contact was almost a stare; she spoke exceptionally slowly, and she kept her arms folded in front of her to communicate that she meant business. I knew that my mother's demeanor and posture meant that she was uncomfortable, but Ms. Applegate didn't know. Ms. Applegate explained that she meant no harm, but she thought that I was acting belligerent when I corrected her.

I did not know what belligerent meant, but I knew it was bad because my mother was visibly upset. Again I knew Momma was bothered, but Ms. Applegate did not. She concealed her frustration well, but I knew that Ms. Applegate was three seconds away from being slapped. I just nervously watched the interaction because I didn't know what else to do. I could tell that my mother and my teacher were equally unsure and uncomfortable with the exchange, and so I was relieved when the meeting was finally over. Whew! Even though I did not understand the implication of everything that took place, my five-year-old body felt the pressure and I spent a lot of time in the restroom that day.

When we ate dinner that night, my parents explained that some White people did not appreciate Blacks defending themselves. They further explained that some Blacks were labeled as troublemakers if they confronted and challenged the actions or words of Whites. I knew what troublemaker meant, and I promised my parents that I would not cause trouble at school. I promised them that I would be on my "church behavior," use my good manners, and follow the rules. I could tell that my parents were troubled about me attending the school, but I was honestly feeling great. I was just excited about hearing the correct pronunciation of my name and replying by saying "present" during the classroom roll call.

On the third day of school, I ran to class and noticed a new person. I was so excited because the person looked like me—brown faced, same texture hair, same Vaseline on the knees, and everything. I ran over to the new student and introduced myself. Her name was Miriam, and we instantly bonded; it was unspoken, but we knew it was us against them. For the rest of the day, we talked, ate, and played together. I felt relieved to finally have someone to play with too. The other girls sometimes allowed me to play with them, but when I did, I always had to be ***it*** when we played hide and seek. Now I did not have the chase the White girls around the playground during recess, I had a Black friend to play with.

Everything was great at school for many months. My sister and mother had taught me my ABCs, how to count to ten and my colors, so I felt extremely smart. Even though Ms. Applegate never picked me or Miriam to answer questions in class, I never became upset. I just figured that the teacher could not see us because she assigned me and Miriam to sit in the last row in the classroom. When we sat in a circle, Miriam and I would have to sit in the end. When the students had to hold hands, she did not require the White kids to hold our hands. We were not treated like the other kids, but for some reason, I never expected the same treatment. I was resigned to being separate, and as long as I wasn't being picked on or called names, I was happy.

Around Christmas time, our class painted pictures for our parents. I was so excited because I made my mother a handprint out of clay, and I felt proud that I had one of the biggest hands in the class. After we finished our projects, I washed my hands and sat down next to Miriam for story time. Ms. Applegate told me to move, and I refused. I explained that I wanted to sit next to Miriam. She told me to move again, and I sighed and pouted for a few seconds. After a few moments of feeling sorry for myself, I quickly jumped up to move. Suddenly I fell to the ground and felt a sharp pain in my forehand. What happened? I was stunned! When I looked up at Ms. Applegate, she was red as a beet. I immediately started crying, not from the pain but from fear. I was emotionally paralyzed. I honestly thought that Ms. Applegate was going to kill me. For the rest of the day, I sat silently, scared to death and shocked by the experience. I was so frightened because I did not understand why Ms. Applegate hit me in the head with a chair. I was petrified. What if she hit me again? And most of all, what did I do?

When my mother arrived home from work, I told her that Ms. Applegate had hit me in the head with a chair. To my surprise, my mother believed me. I was sure that Momma would call me a liar and be convinced that the knot on my head was the result of me fighting at school. But she didn't. I guess she knew that a five-year-old did not have the capacity to make up such an unbelievable story. My mother told me to explain exactly what happened. I told her that Ms. Applegate told me to move, and when I started to move, she hit me in the head with a chair. My mother looked at me with tears in her eyes and told me everything will be okay. She tried to comfort me, but her tears revealed her own worry and sadness. I was not sure if her tears were the result of hearing about my "attack", or her sense of powerlessness, or her apprehension about having another anxiety-provoking exchange with my teacher, or the result of the constant emotional wear and tear of racism or a combination of everything. As I watched my mother cry, I cried to deal with the discomfort of seeing her cry. I did not have the maturity to comprehend her pain, but I knew that I was hurting so I guessed that she was hurting too. Again she promised to go to school with me the following day to speak with my teacher. She put some ice in a facecloth to reduce the swelling on my head and told me to go to bed.

Ms. Applegate was almost trembling when she saw my mother. She nervously explained that I had not obeyed her directions and that she felt that I was so upset that I was attempting to attack her. My mother was incredulous. She was outraged; and it was obvious that Momma was trying to restrain her anger, hurt, and fear. Ms. Applegate apologized, but I could see and sense that something more was going on for both women. I was not sure if it was mutual contempt, unbridled fear, uncontrolled nervousness, controlled rage, or uncertainty. To me, it felt like it was another standoff, and I started shaking and sweating. The room was filled with many emotions, and the tension was palpable. I knew that both women were communicating with each other even though no words were used. Witnessing the silent exchange was excruciating, and my body wanted to release the pressure caused by watching the no-speaking, no-touching fight. It was combat, a brawl, or a battle for sure; but it was nothing that I had ever seen before even on TV. I was so scared that I almost urinated right there in the classroom. I wanted to run, hide in the coatroom, cover my face, or hide under the desk; but I could not move. I was paralyzed and deeply affected despite not really understanding the gravity of it all. I am not sure how long the staring match lasted. I was in shock and had lost all track of time.

After our "meeting," Momma grabbed my hand and we left the classroom. She was walking extremely fast, and my little legs struggled to keep up with her. As we left the building, my mother cried, and I was crying too even though at the time I did not totally understand the emotion behind my tears. I sensed something painful had happened and that other things were happening, but my kindergarten mind could not absorb it all. The next day when I returned to school, Ms. Applegate was gone, and I had a new teacher.

I did not understand it then, but I now understand my mother's tears originated from her feelings of powerlessness. She felt powerless to change the racism that protected abusive teachers. She felt powerless to address a school system that refused to recognize that teachers and some White authorities were harboring resentment and anger toward the Black kids who just wanted a good education. She felt powerless to inspire me to learn, yet at the same time, teach me to survive and thrive in the face of constant prejudice and racism. She felt powerless to shield me from the harsh realities of living as a Black person in an unfair and sometimes cruel world. She felt powerless, which made her also feel helpless.

When I look back on my kindergarten experiences, I realized they had a profound effect on my life. School, which was supposed to be a place of positivity, learning, and optimism for children, introduced me to the chilling and destructive reality of racism, bigotry, and hatred. School represented pain—pain I felt from being ignored by my teacher and classmates as well as the pain my parents experienced trying so desperately to protect me from the harsh reality of prejudice. Some may contend that my parents introduced me to racism by not allowing me to speak to Whites. I believe that my parents like most Black parents at that time, tried their best to limit interaction as a way to ensure my survival as well as their own. They could not risk me saying something that could be misinterpreted as offensive because they were keenly aware of the repercussions that could result—loss of job, loss of housing, harassment, personal injury, etc. I now realize that my parents did their best.

It took many years of healing before I could analyze the life-changing experiences of kindergarten. I now understand why Ms. Applegate did not want to address my mother by her last name. She did not respect my mother as her equal and preferred to call Blacks, regardless of their age, by their first names. I believe that she was taught to refer and treat adult Blacks as if they were inferior, as if they were children. I witnessed many teachers as well as other White people in authority refer to my mother by her first name, yet expected my mother to address them with the obligatory mister and missus. This sent a strong message to me that Whites were superior to Blacks, a message that I unfortunately accepted as true for many years. Fortunately, my father constantly taught and reminded me about the significant contributions and inventions made by Black people. If he had not educated me about our rich culture, I would have been embarrassed to be Black while functioning in a White America. Instead of being Black and *proud*, I would have been Black and *ashamed*.

My kindergarten experiences also painfully taught me that some Whites felt that some Blacks were unruly, wild, and devoid of appropriate social graces. So when I abruptly jumped to move, my teacher instantly thought that I was attacking her. Hitting me in the head with a chair was her way of protecting herself from an unruly, untamed wild beast. It painfully demonstrated that despite my ripe old age of five, I was considered a danger, a threat to be reckoned with.

Kindergarten introduced me to new emotions: panic, distress, apprehension, terror, and confusion just to name a few. Even though I did not experience physical abuse, experiencing incessant prejudice was and still is emotional and spiritual abuse. My mind and body felt the trauma that resulted from racism, and my body learned how to survive and cope in unhealthy ways. As a child, I was unprepared to deal with the constant assault on my and my parents' humanity. And even though I could not acknowledge or articulate my pain, my body could and did. I believe that many of the physical ailments that I have as an adult were the result of my inability to manage and make sense of the discrimination that I experienced, witnessed, and endured in my childhood.

Finally, the toughest and most enduring lesson that I learned was that some Whites would accept Blacks only if Blacks played by rules developed, altered, and adjusted as desired by Whites. The school children only agreeing to play with me if I was It, quickly educated me that Blacks were only accepted by Whites if Blacks humbly agreed and abided by unspoken rules. I vividly remember playing hide and seek and being It, and even when I tagged somebody else to be It, the children quickly changed the rules or instantly made up reasons as to why I had to continue to be It. I remembered hysterically crying from frustration and having the other children laugh and taunt me.

Even though the game is not hide and seek**,** I consistently experience the same game in corporate American. As an African American female, I always have to be It; I have to chase White men, White women, and a few Black men to excel. And despite playing by the ever changing rules, the power brokers continue to manipulate the systems and/or invent reasons to prevent Black women from being included in the game. Therefore, I fortunately, yet painfully, realized in my twenties that I needed to be It—chasing the powerbrokers—if I wanted to succeed in a system that was designed to limit and marginalize people who were and are different. So from kindergarten up to now, I have learned that I have to depend on me for my happiness and financial security. I am not saying that I will not work in Corporate America. I am saying that I will depend on *me* for my development, my growth, my sanity, and my worth. My spiritual and emotional wellness are my responsibilities. And I know that I can depend on me, just God and me!

## CHAPTER 2

# Headache and Heartache

DURING THE SUMMER of 1971, my father lost his job at the McDonnell Douglas Plant. I don't remember him even liking his job there; he said it was monotonous even though I had no idea what that meant. Since there were few job prospects, my father decided to pursue his M.Div., Master of Divinity, degree. He said he was "called" to the ministry, even though I was not clear on who called him or how they called him. My father did not drink or smoke, so I surmised that is was probably okay if he became a minister. My friends' fathers were ministers, and they told me that their fathers drank, smoked, and cussed. Many also shared that the parents were mean at home but nice at church; they had two personalities so to speak. Since my father did none of those things and behaved the same at both places, I assumed that it was acceptable for him to be a minister. To be honest, I was somewhat scared of God, and I felt that my father being a minister would require that God constantly watched over us. For many reasons, having God's constant surveillance scared me to death; I knew that my family could not withstand the extra scrutiny, but that is another story.

Eden Theological Seminary accepted my father into their Master of Divinity program, so we moved to Lockwood, Missouri. We lived in the campus's family housing, and we were surrounded by White people. Some were too friendly, which made me uncomfortable. However, others totally ignored us and acted as if we were invisible. I thought, "Ain't these the people trying to do God's work?" I just prayed that if I went to heaven that God would put me on the Black side. Trying to interact with White people was too much work, and it was confusing.

My father started classes, and he was extremely excited. When he came home, we anxiously waited to hear about his first day of school. My only concern was that my dad had Black friends in his class to talk to and to talk with. Even though I had just turned six, I wanted to protect my father from mean White teachers and White students. School, which should have bee a place of learning, was a place of pain and confusion to me. My painf kindergarten experience had left an indelible mark on me emotional that I would not overcome until my early thirties. Kindergarten taug me that being different equated to pain. As a result, I learned how to a shape shifter—a chameleon—when I moved in White circles. I learne and perfected the art of bringing only parts of me as I traveled in th world. And the parts that I brought had to only be the "accepted" par allowed, acknowledged and accepted by the majority group, White peopl I learned how to show up as only a fraction of SharRon. However, th uninvited parts of me rebelled and expressed themselves as anxiety, lack confidence, and self-deprecation.

My father shared that he was the only Black man in his class and my hea sank. "Oh no," I thought, "the class is going to mess with him." I crie myself to sleep at night and prayed for my father to be strong and fo God to give him favor with his teachers. From that day on, I became ver protective of my father and became obsessed about his classes. I was anxiou when he left for school, anxious when he typed his papers, and anxiou about his potential mistreatment from classmates and professors. I was ju anxious! I was a ball of nerves—a walking basket case who nobody notice or had the energy to deal with. Even though I was acting out and behavin differently, nobody seemed to notice or care. I felt alone.

Despite my tears and pleas against going to school, my parents enrolle me into the first grade at Not-Going-to-Reveal-the-Name Elementar School. We were warned that the school had no Black students, but w were forced to attend due to district's new bussing laws. Needless to sa I was terrified. My mother registered me for my class, introduced me t the school principal, and then escorted me to my classroom. Fortunatel my mother stayed with me until the school bell rang; she had to because could not move. I was petrified and I was shaking nervously. I wanted t cry, but tears would not fall. My kindergarten experience had robbed m of my confidence, my innocence, and my voice. All I could do was stan still; I couldn't speak.

When I entered slowly and nervously into my class, my teacher welcome me and asked me my name, but I could not speak. Too afraid to speak, m mother was forced to answer for me. In her White people voice she sai "her name is SharRon, S-H-A-R-R-O N." The entire class turned and said, "Welcome SharRon." I looked at my feet and waved my sweaty palm as *hi*. That small action took all of my strength, and I felt as if I was going to vomit right there in front of the class. Sensing that I was scared, my mother took me into the hallway. She told me that she understood why I was scared, and she tried to convince me that everything would be okay. She tried to convince me the teacher and children were different, and that first grade would be fun. I unsuccessfully tried to convince her that the children and the teacher were the same; they were White. I cried and begged her not to leave me. Trying to assuage my fears were unsuccessful, so my mother tried another approach and said "Girl, don't you embarrass me in front of these White people. Now, go sit down and act like you got some sense." She looked at me, kissed my head, and left. My heart sank. My mother, who I thought was my supporter, abandoned me. I felt lost in a sea of White faces. I was all alone, just God and me.

Most of the first day of school was a blur. I think that I picked the last seat in the third row. Even though I loved sitting in the front of the class at Sunday school, I hated being in the front at elementary school. I actually thought that I could hide in the back row and limit my interaction with my teacher and the other kids. I laugh today at my strategy because I could have not hidden even if I wanted to; I was the tallest and darkest child in the class.

I don't remember what happened in class that day. I don't even remember meeting people even though I am sure that I did. However, I do remember going to lunch and seeing what appeared to be a million White faces staring at me and my sister Chatone. By the looks on their faces, I assumed that Chatone and I were the first Blacks that they had ever seen, or that we were the first Blacks that they had seen in their school. Either way, I felt like a spectacle and my senses were on high alert.

My sister had to sit with her class, and I had to sit with mine. The other kids did not want to sit with me, so I sat alone on the lunch bench. I constantly looked over to my sister for reassuring glances, and she always smiled at me. She appeared to be having fun—something that I wasn't having. During lunch, I managed to let a few words slip from my tongue but not many. I honestly did not know what to say or do. Fear had paralyzed me beyond belief. I wasn't the loud-talking, joke-cracking, fun-loving girl that I was at home. I was just a shell with nothing entering my brain or leaving it. I was an emotional mute.

When I arrived home, I knew that I had to lie about my school experience for my parents' sake. I felt that I had to tell them everything was going well: school was great and the kids loved me. I had no choice, and I knew the truth did not really matter anyway. We were not moving. I had to go to the White school, and my young parents were ill-equipped to offer any assistance to help me process the fear, dread, and anxiety that I was feeling. My honest experience was irrelevant, so I lied and told my parents that everything was great and that I had fun. After I lied to my parents, they were visibly relieved. My mother said, "I told you that everything was going to be okay." What! I felt crushed and almost admitted that I lied because her words cut me like a knife. "Okay," I thought, "if shaking, sweating, crying, almost vomiting, and having the kids ignore you in class constitutes an okay day, I shudder to think what a bad day at school consisted of."

That night, I found myself praying again. "Oh Lord, help me not be scared of my teacher and the White people. Help them to like me. Help my parents protect me." I remembered praying until I cried. I was so emotionally drained from my first day of school that my body and mind begged for rest. I slept soundly and I didn't dream, which was unusual for me.

My mother dropped us off early for school because she was attending nursing school in St. Louis. Even though school did not start until 8:30 a.m., she dropped us off at around 7:45 a.m. because she was enrolled in classes and/or had to do her clinical training at Barnes Hospital. She wanted to be a nurse; and somehow she was able to work, be a parent, and study. The idea of both of my parents attending school was cool because I did not realize that old people could learn. I loved doing homework beside my old parents; because to a six-year-old, a twenty-five-year-old parent was ancient.

In the forty-five minutes that my sister and I had before school started, we learned how to do flips and tricks on the monkey bars. We could turn backwards and forwards. We could turn flips without using our arms. Eventually we became known for our expertise on the money bars, and we always drew a crowd during recess. Attracting attention on the monkey bars is my first memory of my self-esteem returning. The old SharRon hadn't fully resurfaced, but glimpses of my old personality were returning. Even though I was smart, I did not get attention from my teacher and my classmates. However, during recess, I was a star. I was too young to understand that I had reinforced the stereotype of Blacks being athletically superior. I just craved validation, and the monkey bars were my entrée into marginal acceptance. I hate to admit it, but many Blacks are marginally accepted now too due to their athletic prowess, but that's another story.

As my confidence grew, I attempted to participate more in class. I started raising my hand to answer questions, ask questions, and clean off the blackboard. My teacher rarely picked me, but just raising my hand and knowing the answers made me feel included. To me, I was involved; but in reality, I was less than tolerated.

After a few months, I started to wonder if I was invisible like *Casper the Friendly Ghost*. I would talk to people and they would ignore me. I would ask to sit with classmates during lunch, and they would not acknowledge me. I would raise my hand to answer questions and volunteer to read, but I was rarely picked. I was never invited to parties or invited to play during recess. Was I invisible at school? Did people really see me? Was I really there? Was I dreaming? The constant ignoring made me question my existence because all of my experiences pointed to me being invisible and nonexistent. Since I was constantly ignored at school and sometimes at home, I tried to explain and rationalize the lack of acknowledgement. While my dad was studying, I asked, "Daddy, am I invisible like Casper?" He did not turn away from his books to give me any eye contact or to assess the profundity of my question. He said, "You are not a ghost," and he continued studying. Every day after that I tried to remember what he said and to take solace in his words even though my experience convinced me otherwise. Was I invisible? If I wasn't, I prayed to God that people would start "seeing" me. Being consistently ignored had begun to hurt me not only socially but emotionally.

Show-and-tell was every Friday, and the students were allowed to bring things from home to share with the class. I was excited because I wanted to share that my father was getting a master's degree. I did not understand what a master's degree was, but I knew it had to be something important. Every time my father shared that information with other adults, they were impressed, so I figured that my teacher and the students would be impressed also. When it was my turn, I told my class that my father was in college and getting a master's degree. I was proud! When I noticed the amazement in my teacher's eyes, I happily assumed that she was impressed, so I continued with my story. I told the class that my father was the smartest person in his class and that he was going to get a Ph.D. one day and be famous. I wasn't lying either. I was just repeating what my father said. Boy, did I feel proud even though I had no idea what the degrees meant or what the credentials symbolized.

During recess that day, my teacher called me into the classroom. She chastised me for lying about my father and cautioned me about the consequences of lying again. I proudly explained that I was not lying and shared with her that my father was a student at Eden Theological Seminary in Webster Groves. I also told her that my mother was attending nursing school. I was beaming with pride, unaware that she did not share my enthusiasm. She dismissed me, and back to the money bars I went until the bell rang. I felt important, and I felt proud of my parents.

I never thought about the conversation until it was show-and-tell again. I felt concerned because I did not have anything to share. Fortunately, I saw my mother looking at her high school yearbook and got an idea. I would bring my father's first place track ribbons to show. Because I had not asked my parent's permission to take them, I wasn't able to get the true account of what really happened. All I knew was that he won them. Therefore, I decided that I would make up an elaborate story about winning track meets and earning first place ribbons. I was going to say that Daddy was a track star, so I started talking and created an exciting tale. It was a great story, and before long, I got caught up in my lie. I started to feel that Daddy was impressive to me too. After a while, it did not bother me that I was lying. It felt good to make the story up as I went along because I was able to add colorful details. It felt good seeing and feeling that people were interested in what I had to say. I felt important, and the feeling was intoxicating.

While sharing my elaborate untruth, I passed around my father's blue ribbons for the class to see. I then told them that my father was a well-known track star, a state champion. I knew that part was true because I had heard that mentioned before. But then I started really embellishing, really lying. I said that my father went to the Olympics and that he was an international track star. The more I talked, the better the story sounded, the prouder I became, and the more I lied. Just seeing the students' eyes light up encouraged me to go on. If the teacher was really listening, it would have been obvious that what I said didn't make sense and was highly unlikely. And if she had asked me one question about what I shared, she could have easily exposed me as a fraud. But she did not ask me anything even though she asked the other students questions about what they shared. Like I stated earlier, I was accustomed to receiving less, and sometimes less meant less interest and concern about what I said, did, and offered in class.

After lunch, I started feeling guilty. I was also scared because I was taught that lighting strikes liars. I was afraid and I wanted to confess. I wanted to tell my teacher that I had exaggerated most of the details and invented the others, but for some reason, she did not chastise me for lying like she did before. Since nobody knew or mentioned my first attempt at fiction, I apologized to God and promised not to lie again.

The next few months passed uneventfully. My confidence grew, my grades were above average, and I made one friend, Lisa. The other kids did not like Lisa and always called her "White trash." I did not know what "White trash" meant, but I felt horrible that she was referred to as garbage. When I got home, I asked my mother why Whites called each other "White garbage." I could not remember that it was not garbage, that it was "trash." Nevertheless, my mother said that I should never repeat that phrase again. She explained that referring to a White person as White trash was similar to Blacks referring to each other as niggers. Wow! I was shocked. I thought that all Whites loved each other.

On a Wednesday during spring, I was playing on the monkey bars by myself. Since I often played alone, I was extremely vigilant about my surroundings. On that particular day, three third-grade boys came and taunted me. They called me monkey girl, ape girl, and nigger. My parents had advised me to never address prejudice physically and to be calm if I was outnumbered. Crazy advice to give a kid, but it was helpful. I also wasn't too concerned because I was confident that I could whip each one of them if they messed with me. Thanks to my Uncle Claude, I knew how to fight so I did not panic. I just continued flipping and enjoying myself. Without any warning, I was pushed from behind. I suddenly fell and hit my head on the concrete. I could not see or make out what was happening, but I heard the three boys laughing.

I don't remember much after that because everything was blurry. I could not see and I could not catch my balance. After a few minutes, a crowd gathered around as I desperately tried to stand up. Nobody extended their hand to me, nobody helped. My sister finally saw me and screamed. She ran over to me and put my arm over her shoulder. She tried her best to help me up, but I outweighed her by twenty or so pounds. After hearing the commotion, a playground aide rushed over to me. He picked me up and took me to the nurse's office.

After I was rushed to the nurse's office, the boys admitted to pushing me off the monkey bars. They told the principal that they were only playing with me and that it was not their intention to make me fall. Of course, little White boys don't lie. None of them received any punishment or any disciplinary action. But me, I suffered a mild concussion and never received an apology. No adult said a word. The message was loud and clear—it was acceptable for Whites to injure Blacks without consequences.

When I finally woke up, it was 3:00 p.m. and my mother and the nurse were staring at me. I felt drugged and my head pounded miserably. My mother asked the nurse and the principal what happened. They both said that I "fell" from the monkey bars before school started. My mother was livid, and said, "Why wasn't I notified earlier? She may be seriously hurt." The nurse explained that from what she understood, Blacks had harder heads so she did not see any reason to alarm my mother about the fall. I instantly felt sick, and I suddenly had a Ms. Applegate flashback. This time my mother was composed as she spoke to the nurse and the principal. She promised them that they would pay for not contacting her sooner. She explained that their decision not to seek medical attention jeopardized my safety and health.

While attending seminary, my father had secured a position with Project Equality, a watchdog organization for equal rights. With the backing of Project Equality, my father was able to obtain an apology for me. But more importantly, he was able to change the school zoning laws which allowed more Blacks and low-income Whites to be bussed into the school system.

My father had left his mark on the community, and the racism and injustice at the school were exposed.

I was not able to attend school for a few days after my "falling" incident. When I returned, nobody said a word to me or inquired about my injury. I knew that the teachers were aware that I had been hurt, and the big swollen knot on my head was visible for everyone to see. It was obvious that something had happened, yet no one mentioned the knot, no one expressed any empathy to me, and no one appeared concern. Why should they? I was just a first-grade Black girl with a plum-size knot on her head. I was just a Black girl who was terrorized by three White boys. I was just a Black girl who was so insignificant that the school nurse had not notified her mother about a fall that could have risked her health. Why should the White staff, teachers, and students acknowledge such an injustice? I was just an unwanted and unwelcomed Black girl in a school previously reserved for Whites only.

I also now ask myself why the teacher assumed that I was lying about my father's academic excellence, but did not question me when I lied about his athletic ability. Probably in her mind, blacks being able to run and jump were acceptable; it was expected. However, Blacks being intelligent and being accepted to one of the most prestigious theological schools in the state was unbelievable. I thank God that I was too naive to understand the implications of my teacher's concern.

I often ask myself why and how did a medical professional succumb to prejudicial thoughts about Blacks despite being trained and educated otherwise. How did that happen? I have come to understand that racism is so embedded in the psyche and so reinforced by society that even objective information can be disregarded. So to bigots, science means nothing. Their racist beliefs reign.

Suffering a mild concussion and nobody assuming responsibility taught me a few things. First, always be aware of my surroundings so that I can escape. Secondly, be mindful of the emotional states of people around me in order to anticipate their actions so that I can ensure my safety. And finally, always have an alternative and/or escape plan to minimize physical and psychological injuries. The concussion had left an indelible mark on my life and catapulted me to a childhood depression that I did not understand

and could not process. I just felt powerless and felt outnumbered. I did not have anybody to protect me at school—not on the school yard, lunchroom, or classroom. I also could not understand how me and my pain were so invisible to others because the pain and my broken spirit were so palpable to me. I prayed and tried to remind myself that I had to depend on me as I traveled through a dangerous, prejudicial White America. I also realized that racial oppression had left some Blacks impotent, and depending on Black America to protect me was also fruitless. I could not articulate my feelings, but I somehow knew that I could depend on me, just God and me. I just prayed that God would not let me down.

## CHAPTER 3

# Trying to Fit In

ANOTHER SCHOOL YEAR, another school. It was no wonder why I was not anticipating returning to school in September after my first two years of instructional hell. I was not excited, but I was at least happy that I was not returning to Concussion Elementary School, a school where I learned the meaning of severe head pain. Instead, I was going to another elementary school—a school that I hoped would have more people who looked like me, Black people.

All summer long, I was extremely defiant. I picked fights with my sister, argued with my parents, was disrespectful to my neighbors, contrary at church. I was angry—angry for feeling humiliated by White teachers, angry at being ignored by White classmates, angry for not performing well in school, angry for not defending myself when classmates called me names, and angry at my parents for moving us into an integrated, but really segregated, community. I was angry! And I had no one to help me understand my feelings. I had no one to process my pain so I just acted out. I just fought and argued with anyone or everyone who crossed my path. I was hurting; and even though I could not articulate my pain, my spirit knew the depths of it. I needed help and guidance, but my behavior discouraged any attempt from others to help me, love and comfort me. To others, I must have looked like a wounded animal waiting to attack.

During the summer, I developed a deep resentment toward my older sister, Chatone. To me, she was beautiful and smart, and all grown-ups liked her. They commented about her good behavior, her good looks, and her academic achievements. White people even liked her, yet sent subtle messages that they did not like me. Maybe I was sending negative vibes to them which prevented them from liking me. Who knows? And if I was sending negative vibes, I really did not want to act mean or aloof toward Whites. I was just scared. To me, Whites were people who just existed to hurt me; not people in whom I could depend on or trust.

Not visiting my Black friends from our old neighborhood prolonged the summer. It was the first summer without much double Dutch rope, dodge ball, kick ball, and jacks. When my mother wasn't studying, which wasn't too often, she played double Dutch rope with us. We would have a great time saying rhymes, jumping rope, and having jumping contests. Even though I enjoyed jumping rope with my family, I became irritated when some White people would stare at us. It felt as if they were watching us, and I wasn't sure if they were watching to learn or watching to harm. Anyway, I hated it! I hated feeling like a spectacle.

I became irritated when White girls with no rhythm tried to play with us too. They couldn't jump, and heaven forbid if they tried to turn the rope to the beat. Most of the time, I would just leave because I always grew too frustrated to show them how to jump and/or turn the rope. Patient Chatone stayed to teach them and, boy, did she get it when she got home. As soon as she stepped inside the door, I would beat her up or try to beat her up for showing the White children how to play a Black game. I did not think that I was being unfair or prejudiced. I just instinctively knew that if the shoe was on the other foot, the White children would not have allowed us to play with them. I had been excluded too many times, and I did not feel that I had to appease the White kids during my summer break. Trying to pacify them and assimilate with them during the school year was torture enough. I refused to participate; and since my sister felt differently, I distanced myself from her.

When the first day of school finally rolled around, I was not excited. I had not begged my parents for new school clothes, a lunch box, or anything. The only person I begged anything from was God, and I only begged God for peace and safety. I just wanted to have a school year with friends, no fights, and no fractures. I just wanted to go to school, grit my teeth and get the school year over with.

When the school bell rang, I attempted to go to the seats in the back of the class also known as the Black seats, but the teacher had assigned seats alphabetically. I felt nauseous as I realized that my seat was in the third row and was the third chair. I did notice, however, that the school was more integrated. They had all types of people—Black, White, Chinese, and some types of Brown people. The Brown people were new to me because I did not know how to categorize them; my world was either Black or White with a few Asians sprinkled in. There were also some kids that wore beanie hats on their heads. I thought that they were affiliated with the Boy Scouts, but I later learned that they were Jewish. I had never seen Jews before, and I honestly couldn't tell the difference. They looked White to me, and so that's how I classified them, not Jewish, just white.

My greatest surprise and joy was seeing Black teachers. At first, I thought they were the cleaning ladies or lunchroom ladies because those were the only professions that I saw black women do in schools. But I knew that they had to be somebody important because they wore beautiful dresses and wore lipstick. Unfortunately, I did not have a black teacher; but the girl with all of the luck, my sister, did. Her name was Ms. Johnson, and she was beautiful! She talked like the White teachers and had a great White people voice. But, I could still detect that she had soul. Her speech had rhythm.

My nonchalant feeling toward school showed in my average grades. Usually, I was an above-average student and always received As and Bs. Now, I was lucky to earn Cs in most subjects. My parents were alarmed, but there was nothing that they could do. Neither punishments nor threats encouraged me to apply myself. I wasn't motivated to learn, and I seldom participated in class. I just wanted the teacher to ignore me to ensure that I would not have any more embarrassing and painful moments. But at the same time, I longed for the teacher's attention and wanted to feel loved and accepted. It was a challenging dichotomy. I wanted to be part of the crowd, but I had no idea how to deal with the daily fear of constant rejection and alienation. My biggest regret is that my parents didn't seek therapy for me. But therapy was not something that Black families, especially my family, believed in. My parents' therapy consisted of getting the beat down if I did not change my behavior, and punishment and extra chores if I failed to improve my grades. That was it! So I had two therapy alternatives: belt on my behind and/or extra time in the prayer line. My parents were convinced that those alternatives were the only solutions despite their limited effectiveness on me.

By the second semester, I had successfully proven the stereotype that many White teachers had about Blacks students—that we were incapable of exceling academically. I did not believe that stereotype myself, but I am sure that my lackluster performance confirmed whatever preconceived notions that my teacher had.

My school goals were to make sure that I was not the center of any more controversies, fights, or fits. I did not want to subject my parents, especially my mother, to any more stressful events. I owed them that much. Also, I just couldn't bear to see my mother cry again because of me and school, so I checked into school physically and checked out mentally. To me, I was being safe.

The smartest girl in class was a Chinese girl named Sunglee. She always made perfect scores in her tests, and her homework was always completed in the mornings. I envied her so much, but not enough to consistently do my own homework or study. I tried miserably to be her friend, but she ignored me. She only played with the White children, and it appeared that the White children accepted her too. The White children accepting her baffled me because I was never accepted when I was the only Black girl. I was stunned and jealous of her acceptance, and I felt resentful toward her. I wanted to be accepted, I wanted to be played with, I wanted to be invited to parties, I wanted to share my lunch, and I wanted to be included. But I wasn't, and I tried to make peace with being on the sidelines and existing on the periphery. But every failed attempt to be included chipped away at my fragile and constantly declining self-esteem.

The following Sunday, I asked my Sunday school teacher why the White children played with Sunglee and not me. She said that she did not know for sure, but she thought that maybe White children thought that Blacks were dangerous or something. I was shocked! Dangerous, why? I started to cry and explained that I wasn't dangerous, and that I wanted to be like the other kids at school. Instead of consoling me or being empathic, she reminded me of how hard life was for her growing up. She shared her experiences dealing with the Klan, and how her father was almost killed by a White mob. By the time I left Sunday school, I was visibly shaken. I was now more fearful than ever before. Will I ever have to deal with the Klan? Will my father be assaulted by a mob at his school? My Sunday school teacher had unknowingly increased my anxiety by a hundred fold. When I returned to school, I found it harder to listen, harder to concentrate. I was on high alert because I knew little about the Klan; and before my Sunday school teacher shared her experiences, I wasn't aware that the Klan killed people. I was traumatized, frightened, and terrified for me and my family. I needed help and I needed hope, but I got neither. It was obvious that my Sunday school teacher needed therapy too because she did not have enough sense not to scare the Jesus out of me.

I excelled at sports; and as a result, I was invited to participate in various games during PE. I was proud of earning a reputation for something else besides being a mediocre student with little communication skills. In every sport I played, my team or I would win. My teacher, who basically ignored me in class, soon started picking me to be the team captain for the sports teams. Eventually, the children also started to see that I was good at something—sports. I had no idea that I was proving another widely-held stereotype about Black people. I was just happy to be included and noticed, and so I smiled like Steppin Fetchit (a degrading caricature of Black people) and reveled in the compliments about my athletic prowess. I was too young and ignorant to understand what I was doing. And I was too emotionally needy to understand and appreciate the impact of my behavior on me and other Black students. Unknowingly, I had become the Black jock and the sports mascot for the class. The price of being included by the White students and teacher was marginalization and devaluation. The sad part was that I allowed it to happen. Had I performed well in school, I could have challenged the myth. But emotionally and spiritually, I was spent. Surviving in a what-felt-like hostile environment with no support system was overwhelming.

Sunglee unknowingly proved a widely accepted stereotype that all Asians were smart. Just like the teacher picked me for the team captain in sports, Sunglee was picked to lead all of the academic events. She was the team captain for the spelling bee, history contests, and the math contests. The rest of the class never complained about Sunglee's selection as a leader; however, they did complain about me leading the basketball, soccer, and volleyball teams. Why? Despite my ability, maybe their parents taught them that Blacks were subservient, or maybe they had Black maids and butlers and had grown accustomed to seeing Blacks in inferior roles and positions. I am not sure. All I know and all I experienced were constant rejection and struggle. Struggle to be included, struggle to be accepted, and struggle to conceal my constant rejection. As the school year continued on, it was harder to conceal my rejection, and I would often cry in class. I cried so often that the students and teacher became immune to my tears. I felt alone.

Together, Sunglee and I had successfully validated the erroneous stereotypes about our races—Blacks are good athletes and Asians are smart. Both stereotypes were equally damaging because it allowed children and teachers to label us and others like us, which denied us our individuality. It also prevented us from pursuing other interests. Since we were different and wanted to be accepted by the majority group, we had to maintain our exceptional skills in our prescribed and designated areas. For me, that meant spending valuable time becoming proficient at sports rather than concentrating on academics. And maybe for her, it meant spending an exorbitant amount of time studying and not enjoying other childhood activities.

Overall, another school year and another failed attempt at fitting in. I learned an important lesson though—I could get attention and acceptance if I excelled at something, so I vowed to apply myself at my next school. I wanted to be celebrated for my sports achievement and my academic ability. I did not know how I was going to earn exceptional grades, and I did not know how I was going to deal with classmates ignoring me, but I was determined to get noticed and be included. It was up to me, just God and me.

## CHAPTER 4

# Educational Ecstasy

I SPENT ANOTHER boring summer at Eden Theological Seminary. No new Black friends to play with, no Black history books in the local libraries, and no neighborhood stores that carried the snacks that I had grown to enjoy. Even though I did not especially enjoy visiting my sanctified, ultraconservative grandparents, I was excited about having access to Black kids and access to dill pickles with peppermint sticks shoved in the middle, pig ears with hot sauce, and tripe sandwiches drowned in mustard. Sometimes my Aunt Rita and Uncle Claude took us to White Castle to get fart burgers—small hamburgers smothered with onions and pickles. Boy, I was in junk food heaven, and I had an additional fifteen pounds to show for it when I returned to school.

During the summer, my mother had transferred us to McKnight Elementary School, which was the third school that I attended in eighteen months. Between redistricting, bussing, and my parents trying to help us escape classroom racism, I had no stability. And since the only thing that was stable and certain was being ignored and invisible, changing schools stopped affecting me. I had checked out emotionally and academically, so in many ways I was numb. To me, a new school just meant familiar pain.

But that year, I was almost interested about returning to school because McKnight was located in an integrated community. I was also extremely excited about having an opportunity to interact with people who looked like me—Black people. Since I had so many negative experiences in predominately White schools, my mother was desperately trying to prevent any more negative racial occurrences. She was also very concerned about my education since my grades and my enthusiasm for learning had dropped. She hoped that a more diverse environment would restore my passion for reading, writing, and arithmetic. My parents were encouraged too because my teacher was Black and was committed to teaching Black history.

My parents were also concerned about my little brother Patrick. After witnessing the dramatic effect that school racism and isolation had on me, my parents felt compelled to ensure that my brother's classroom environment was more conducive to learning and infused with positivity. At that time, new research revealed that Blacks boys had a harder time in elementary school due to teacher neglect and teacher misinformation. As a result, ensuring that my brother's teachers were not only able but willing to give him adequate time, attention, and instruction was paramount.

My class at McKnight Elementary consisted of twenty-five children, with eleven of them Black. For the first time at school, I felt invigorated as I rushed to introduce myself to my Black classmates. Introducing myself to Black children was so revitalizing because I instantly felt accepted and affirmed by them. Their acceptance boosted my confidence so much that I was even excited about introducing myself to the White children. It was amazing how my confidence grew just knowing that I was no longer outnumbered and viewed differently. I felt powerful, and for some reason, I knew that this school was going to be different.

My teacher's name was Mrs. Eldridge. She was brown skinned and had brown hair. She also had green eyes that made her face glow. But most of all, she always wore a smile. I knew that she smiled at everybody, but I always felt that she smiled exceptionally wide at me. I guess I needed to believe that she cared more about me than she did the other kids. I had felt neglected for so long that just having any potential to feel *seen* started to heal the emotional and spiritual wounds from my earlier years.

As the school year continued, my parents noticed a difference in my attitude. My old fun-loving, fast-talking, joyful personality had returned, and I was now a student who was excited about learning. I quickly became the class clown, but I was never disrespectful because I did not want to jeopardize my relationship with Ms. Eldridge. For the first time in three years, I felt confident enough to complete my homework, answer questions in class, and excel in non-sporting events. I even volunteered to clean the erasers, empty the classroom trashcans, and clean out my desk. I was hungry for acceptance, and I did everything I could to gain and keep Ms. Eldridge's attention and support. Her approval was everything to me. I was seen, and being seen was healing, liberating, and affirming.

I received my first invitation to a birthday party. Before McKnight, I was never invited to parties or play dates. I painfully remembered children returning to school on Mondays talking about the fun that they had at so-and-so's party. I would almost cry as the children talked about the games they played, the food they ate, and the toys they won. The children would talk about their fun right in front of me as if I were invisible. I tried to pretend their party talk didn't affect me, but it did. I really wanted to be invited to parties, and I never understood why I was the only person that never received an invitation. But this was to change, and, boy, was I excited. I was going to have fun.

Laura Reid was turning nine and she invited me, SharRon, to help her celebrate! The week of the party, I was a nervous wreck. I worried because I wanted to bring the perfect present and wear the perfect outfit. I even begged my mother to let me wear my hair down, which was something that was reserved for Sundays. To me, Laura's party was my coming-out event, the evidence I needed to know that I was finally accepted by other children. I know that Laura had no idea what her invitation meant to me, and I still reminisce about walking in her house, dancing with the other kids, playing pin-the-tail-on-the-donkey, prancing down the Soul Train line. Sometimes I still visualize the look on Laura's face when she opened the gift I gave her. She loved the purse and the Charlie perfume. Laura loving my present made me feel loved too.

After the party, Laura and I became best friends. We always played together, ate together, talked together, etc. We even helped each other with our homework and art projects. Every Sunday, I thanked God for Laura, Mrs. Eldrige, and McKnight Elementary School. I was finally enjoying life, making friends, feeling accepted, and getting good grades. I was being *me* with God's help, just me.

The fourth grade was truly a turning point in my life. My confidence in my ability to learn and compete academically with other students was restored. More importantly, my fear of White people decreased. I no longer felt that all Whites hated and wanted to harm Blacks. I had experienced their friendship and acceptance. I had finally experienced an environment where everybody, Blacks and Whites, got along. We played together, sat together, and laughed together. What a refreshing, and life changing, experience for me!

I shudder to think what would have happened if I continued to have negative racial experiences. I wonder if I would have completely withdrawn from learning or from interacting with White people, and I wonder if I would have become violent in an attempt to let Whites feel my pain, anger, and heartache. The most destructive thing that could have occurred is that I could have become a statistic and stereotypical Black—a Black violent underachiever. A Black violent underachiever created by racism, neglect, and isolation. Of course, some Whites could suggest that they played no role in creating such an unfortunate, painful situation. They could argue that Black children were not raised properly by Black parents, that Black children had inferior intelligence, and that Black children lacked the capacity to excel in school. Some Whites could even suggest that Whites played no role in my painful years of school despite the numerous slurs I endured, the racial isolation that I experienced, the neglect that I received from my teachers, and the fear that I felt when I was unable to protect myself and my parents from emotional and physical pain that resulted from my attendance in school. I am grateful for changes, transitions, and shifts. Without them, my life would have been limited, listless, and lackluster.

Through it all, I knew that I could depend on God, my parents, and me. But mostly, just God and me!

## CHAPTER 5

# The Color of God

MY EDUCATIONAL ECSTASY was short-lived due to the bishop appointing my father to a church in East St. Louis, Illinois. My father was extremely happy about his appointment because a church appointment regardless of size was supposedly a sign of personal and spiritual maturity. My father was one of the youngest ministers in the African Methodist Episcopal Church, and he felt that he needed to prove himself to the organization even if meant moving his family to yet another city.

I received my father's announcement with anger, fear, and grief. Anger because I could not understand how my father could consider moving us after the tumultuous years I had endured at school. I felt fear because I knew that another school could bring more problems, pests, and pain. I felt grief as I mourned the loss of my friends, Ms. Eldrige, McKnight School and especially, Laura. To me I was losing the only environment that made me feel special, loved and accepted—an environment I never thought that I would have again.

In the cold of January, we packed our belongings and moved to Edgemont, Illinois. I secretly kept a special box to remember my friends and experiences at McKnight. I packed Laura's birthday invitation, my first A+ book report entitled "Mr. Soul Robot" that my mother helped me write, and my Halloween photographs so that I could remember the faces of my many friends. My sister said that I was stupid for keeping "junk," but to me it was a treasure. It was the only evidence that confirmed that I mattered and that I was "seen."

The East St. Louis Public School System was pitiful. We heard accounts of classroom violence, outdated textbooks, inattentive teachers, under-funded programs, etc. Upon hearing such horror stories, my parents enrolled us into St. Phillips Catholic School. I didn't know much about Catholicism except that they had a pope. Other than that, I did not know what to expect; however, I did anticipate experiencing discrimination. Prejudice was one of the constants in my life so I expected it, I anticipated it, and I did my best to emotionally prepare for it. The only thing that prevented me from having another emotional new school breakdown was that the school was supposedly a religious school. Believe me, I prayed that the teachers and students had the same understanding of God and God's ways that I had. Without a shared theology, I knew that I was toast.

When we registered for school, we were greeted by a lady named Sister Gail. I was accustomed to calling women Sisters at my church and so using the same greeting at school gave me a sense of security. After meeting Sister Gail, we toured the campus and went to Mass. Now Mass was strange! First of all, there were no instruments except an acoustic guitar. At my church, we used drums, guitars, pianos, organs, tambourines, etc. I had always associated church with instruments and singing, so Mass was extremely unsettling to me. All of the kneeling, standing, sitting action annoyed me too. I wanted to yell, "Man, make up your mind," but my mother would have ended my life on the spot. The sermon was also boring and delivered in a monotone fashion. I couldn't believe that the minister just talked. He didn't even get excited nor jump. Nobody said "Amen," "Praise God," "Preach, preacher," or anything. I thought that if the minister showed some excitement, the congregation would get with him and back him with "amens" and some "praise the Lords". But no, he was humdrum and I was dumbfounded. I just couldn't believe my eyes or my ears. Was this really church?

At the end of church or mass, the people went up to take communion. I thought this was blasphemous because it wasn't the first Sunday of the month. Heck, it wasn't even Sunday, it was a school day. I knew that everybody else knew that you only took communion on the first Sunday of the month unless it was a special occasion. I trembled in the pews because I knew God was going to show His disappointment at these wayward people called Catholics. I was outdone, and I and started to pray and ask the Lord to spare me. I also reminded God that I wasn't Catholic just in case He wanted to punish them.

I was too disturbed about Mass to enjoy my first day of school. I just couldn't believe the church service that I attended. I just knew that the people could not have been "saved" acting like that. I always remember hearing that people who really loved God should enjoy worshipping with song and praises, and I knew that the people who attended Mass in the morning could not have enjoyed such a boring service. I knew that they were not saved and that hell was their destination. And since they were going to hell, I was going to skip as many services as I could just in case God sent lightning.

Since my father was working on his theology degree, I inquired about Catholics as soon as he got home. I told him that Catholics did not know how to "have church." I explained to him that attending Mass would endanger my life because I knew that God was not pleased with their kind of worship. My father laughed at me and told me that Catholics were Christians too, but they prayed and worshipped differently. When I asked why, my father gave me a long theological lesson that I didn't understand or listened to completely. I just secretly vowed to pray for Catholics because I felt sorry for them. I really wanted them to have fun at church and have fun in heaven.

My conversation with my dad did alleviate some of my fears—at least I did not feel scared about being in a Catholic cathedral anymore. My father convinced me that Catholics were saved and explained that God, and only God, will determine who is praising and serving Him/Her appropriately and earnestly. My father thought that he was putting me in my place, but I honestly felt relieved to know that I personally didn't have to pray all the Catholics into heaven. His explanation was definitely a weight off my shoulders.

Grieving over my friends at McKnight prevented me from getting close to people. I was always friendly towards my classmates and teachers, but my heart was broken. I missed my friends miserably. I also feared becoming close to anyone because my father explained that his assignment in East St. Louis was temporary. He was unable to define temporary, which made me even more reluctant to initiate any friendships with the other students.

My grades suffered too. I received and only worked for Bs and Cs. I really didn't care about school. My parents were too busy anyway. My father worked a full-time job, attended school full time, and pastored a church on the weekends. My mother worked full time, and many times overtime, attended nursing classes, and became the overly involved pastor's wife.

Nobody really cared about us, at least that's how I felt. We were on our own to process the move, process Catholicism, and process raising ourselves without much parental supervision.

My parents took notice of my declining grades after I received a D in science, Cs in my other classes and an Unsatisfactory in music. To my dismay, my father questioned my grade in music first because he knew I could read and play the piano beautifully. You see, I was forced to be one of his church musicians, and he wanted to ensure that I was learning how to play better. Boy, I was extremely upset when I realized that my father was more concerned about me not being able to read music for his church than my poor performance at school. He later apologized but I did not care. I realized what was more important to him—me as his church musician, not me as his academically underachieving daughter. I did not know it then but my father's promotions in the denomination were directly linked to increasing church attendance. Even if he explained that to me, I would not have understood nor cared. To a child accustomed to feeling ignored and being ignored, any action or word that confirmed my feelings of inadequacy was potent and emotionally deadly.

Sister Susan, my science teacher, took a special interest in me for reasons I still don't know. Maybe she saw my sadness or maybe she was just a caring an adult who felt compassionate. Who knows? Sometimes I think God told her that I needed someone to pay attention to me; someone to validate my existence. She tutored me for two months and desperately tried to increase my enthusiasm about science and learning. It worked because I improved most of my grades to Bs by the end of the school term.

After I became accustomed to attending Mass at 7:30 in the morning, I began to enjoy the silence. Even the acoustic guitar didn't annoy me as much; however, the boring sermons were murder. During the forty minute service, I frequently found myself daydreaming about my friends at McKnight. I wondered if the girls were playing double Dutch rope and jacks. I wondered if the boys were playing dodge ball. Many times I was actually able to imagine myself running around in the playground with my friends. Morning Mass was my quiet time, and reminiscing made the services and my life bearable.

On one of the rare days that I was paying attention at Mass, I realized something that I never saw before. I realized that all the statues on the wall and those painted on the windows were white. I also realized that all the sisters and fathers were White. I was so accustomed to seeing White authority figures that I never before questioned why no Black person was a leader in the Catholic Church. After Mass, I knew I had to ask Sister Susan why there were no Black or yellow faces on the walls or windows even if it meant punishment for me.

After Mass I marched up to Sister Susan and said, "Why ain't there any Black people on the walls at the cathedral?" Sister Susan was so stunned at the indignation in my voice that she almost yelled back at me. However, in her most restrained voice, she explained that the so-called people on the walls were saints. She also said that there were Black and Spanish saints. Again I asked her with my hands on my imaginary hips, "Why ain't some of them on the wall?" By this time, Sister Susan had begun to lose her poise. Something told me that she wasn't angry at me, but she felt uncomfortable because she did not have an answer. I also knew she resented being questioned by an eleven-year-old.

Realizing that no answer would have satisfied me, Sister Susan reminded me that God loves all people and that it shouldn't matter if only Whites were on the wall. I said, "If it doesn't matter, why aren't there any Black people on the windows." She was exasperated and I knew but I did not care. I was frustrated too. I explained to her that my father removed all of the pictures of White Jesus at his church because he felt that Blacks seeing only White representations of Christ perpetuated the inferiority of Blacks. Of course, I didn't understand what I said, nor was I confident that I quoted my father accurately. I just knew that my father was smart, and if he said something similar to what I repeated to Sister Susan, it was profound. Mentally exhausted from dealing with an agitated student, Sister Susan offered no more explanations. She just ordered me to my classroom.

When I recounted my conversation with Sister Susan to my parents, my mother sighed. She said "Why do you always have to start trouble?" I explained that I wasn't starting trouble. I just wanted to know why all the statues and saints were White if Black saints existed too. I tried to convince my mother that it wasn't fair since there were Black Catholics that were members of the church too. Fearing another racial incident, my mother pleaded with me to be good—in other words shut up and stop asking so many questions.

My father took another approach. He explained that most religions in America were tainted by Europeans centuries ago. He explained that White painters drew Jesus with blonde hair and blue eyes in contradiction to the Bible. He shared a Bible verse with me that described Jesus as a brown man with hair like wool. To me, hair like wool meant kinky. Immediately, I felt an amazing sense of pride knowing that God was Black even though my father said that most people in that region may have not been Black, just dark skinned due to the sun. It didn't matter what my father said after I saw the verse in the Bible. Jesus was Black to me, which meant that God was Black too. From then on, I start visualizing Jesus and God as dark-skinned Black men with big white Afros and beards. They looked like me—Black.

That night I felt closer to God than ever before. I felt like I was being held by a friend and listened to. It was such an overwhelming feeling that I cried while I was praying. I still don't understand what made me cry, but I knew that God being Black made me feel more loved, accepted and heard. When I thought God was White, I actually felt that I was less important to Him. I felt that my concerns, needs and prayers didn't matter. I actually felt that my prayers were only answered after all of the White people's prayers were answered. Now, I felt that I finally was first in line to speak with God—a soulful Black God.

When I explained my spiritual revelation to my supposedly White friends, they were quick to label me as a racist and bigot, not a Christian. What? I am a bigot because I believe that God is Black. I said, "You are a bigot because you want God to be White." I was ready to argue because God was important to me, and I was going to defend my Black God even if it meant getting expelled. I had to. It was a spiritual life and death situation to me. The debate about the color of God escalated, and Sister Susan tried her best to defuse the situation. But we students were not going to relent; we all defended our opinions forcefully. Sister Susan tried to regain control of the class and even tried to convince me (only me) that it didn't matter what color God or Jesus was. I said, "If it doesn't matter, then he can be Black." I even shared the scripture with them that described Jesus's characteristics They denied that it was true or they attempted to convince me that Jesus was "all colors." In her mind and in the minds of the students, God and Jesus being multicolored or looking like a rainbow was more acceptable than being Black or dark skinned. But it didn't matter to me, God was Black and I was not budging on my opinion.

It was so offensive to me when people adamantly denied or distorted the Bible when it concerns color. During these heated discussions, I consistently reminded them that Jesus's color didn't matter, right? Even though they realized they were being hypocritical, most couldn't conceive of Jesus being anything else other than a White, blond-haired, and blue-eyed man. I honestly feel that if Jesus came back Black, some of my White associates would convert to another religion or opt to go to hell.

So St. Phillips Catholic School was my introduction to racism in religion, an area that I didn't think could be contaminated with prejudice. I was wrong, dead wrong. Despite the revelation that some racists also consider themselves to be Christian, my faith and devotion to God grew because I knew God cared about me—Black God and Black Jesus cared about Black me.

Even though my father cautioned me about saying God was only Black, I knew I had to count on me—my interpretation and depiction of God to experience a deep relationship with God. I had to feel that somebody powerful looked like me and accepted me as a Black child. The deadly sins of racism affected me so significantly that I had to create my own picture of God to survive spiritually. If not, my faith in God would have been destroyed because I could never accept the image of a White God fully loving me because I was Black. I had to depend on me, just God and me.

## CHAPTER 6

# Category Crisis

MY FATHER'S TEMPORARY assignment in East St. Louis lasted one year, and so we relocated again to Brentwood, Missouri. It was a very unfortunate time to move since there were only three more months of school left in the school year. I never understood why we left so abruptly anyway, but I later found out that my father had left the African Methodist Episcopal church and joined the United Methodist Church. I wasn't too upset about leaving St. Phillips AME Church nor the AME denomination because I had never developed any true friendships. But I was tired of packing and repacking our belongings.

Our apartment in Brentwood was beautiful; probably the nicest place we had ever lived. It was supposed to be an integrated neighborhood, which meant that only a few Black families lived there. I had learned to read between the lines when people said "integrated" anything. It still meant predominately White or that White flight had not yet started.

I don't remember the name of the elementary school that I attended. It's difficult to keep track when you keep moving around. I do remember, however, taking a lot of tests on my first day at my new school. I had been through the same ritual every time I went to another school, but something was different about the tests we took that day. The questions were very easy, and the tests were not timed. I really did not mind the difference because I never felt capable of doing my best under pressure, so I welcomed the change.

When I received my test results on the second day of school, I was told that my scores were exceptionally low. This surprised me because even though I was never a rocket scientist, I knew that I had above-average intelligence. The counselor explained that I would need to enroll in class where I could receive additional attention. I didn't mind attention because I loved being the center of the universe. What I didn't understand, however, was that "additional attention" meant being placed into special education classes.

In the late '70s, special education was reserved for physically and mentally handicapped children. To me, it was a place for students that rode the miniature yellow buses and rode around in wheelchairs. It was for the students who were slow learners. I knew that I didn't meet any of those criteria even though I had loafed around in class. Granted, I was not applying myself, but I did not have a learning disability. I was just suffering from a lack of motivation.

I pleaded with the counselor not to put me in the class with the handicapped kids. I realized later it was not politically correct to say things like that, but back then I sure said it. I knew that the other kids in my apartment complex would tease me if I was placed in special education classes, but more importantly, I knew that I didn't belong. My academic ability did not demand placement in such classes.

The counselor walked me to the special education department as tears rolled down my eyes. I cursed myself for being a terrible student in my earlier years. I must have told myself that I hated myself a hundred times before I entered the classroom.

When I entered the department, I was stunned. It was a zoo. Children ran, jumped, and shouted at will. Even though the teachers were there, nobody chastised the kids for acting like animals. Whatever the children wanted to do, they did without fear of any repercussions. I just stood at the entrance crying and asking, "God, why me?" Why did I have to be in the class with the retards? Again, it is not the politically correct to say such things, but I did say it. I said to myself, "Why me, God. Why me?"

As I cried hysterically, I remembered by mother testifying in church about her pregnancy with me. I remember her saying that the doctor told her that I would be born retarded or something due to a lack of oxygen available to my brain. "Oh no," I thought. Maybe I was always retarded, but now it's starting to show. The more I thought about my mother's testimony, the more I cried. Was I really mentally or intellectually delayed? My self-esteem was so low that it was difficult to convince myself that I was capable of performing and that I was not academically deficient.

When I got home, I didn't tell my mother about my placement in special education. I was too embarrassed, and I didn't want to risk dealing with taunts from my sister. I reminded my mother about her testimony, and she confirmed that everything I remembered was true. Her confirmation made me believe that I really was retarded all along and that my poor tests grades were proof.

On the third day of school, I went to class late on purpose. I wasn't trying to be defiant, but I didn't want to risk being seen going into the Special Ed. Department. I almost felt like a spy sneaking around hallways, hiding behind lockers, and running inside indoors to keep my embarrassing secret.

My teacher never assigned work the entire day, and so I just sat and read magazines and drew pictures. To me being in Special Ed. felt more like being at a baby-sitters rather than a classroom. There were no classroom assignments, no reading assignments, no classroom discussions, nothing. The teachers didn't expect anything from the students, and the students were content to deliver nothing.

After about one week of doing absolutely nothing, I checked out books at the library and wrote three book reports on important Black people that I heard about. I read about Frederick Douglas, Harriet Tubman, and George Washington Carver. I would have read more, but the library had few books about Black people, and I wasn't interested in reading about Whites. When I turned in my book reports, my teacher was impressed with my initiative and writing ability, so I had an idea. I would make up homework and complete it to prove that I shouldn't be in Special Ed. In essence, I would teach myself.

I didn't know where to begin, so I secretly copied homework assignments from my sister's books. I secretly copied her math and science problems and worked hard to complete her assignments by myself. Her spelling words were difficult to pronounce and memorize, but I was determined to show my teacher that I was not Special Ed. material. I didn't even feel tempted to copy my sister's answers because I knew that I had to learn the information anyway to pass the necessary tests to return to a normal classroom. I studied, prayed and studied some more. I was scared to give up because I had slowly started accepting the fact that I was retarded, and I knew that I would have to do extra work to maintain the limited intelligence that I thought I had

I was scared that my brain was deteriorating; I felt it was urgent to learn as much as I could as fast I as could.

As I started turning in my own homework assignments, my lazy teacher actually had the nerve to grade my work and put comments on the top of my papers. Boy, that really pissed me off! I thought to myself that this fool didn't have the initiative to give homework, but had the audacity to correct it with red ink. I hated seeing my papers that I worked so hard on marked up and circled in red. My anger subsided though when I remembered my mission, which was to escape from Special Ed.

While I was in Special Ed., I never became friendly with the other students because I thought I was better than they were. I hate to admit it, but that was the way I felt. It was not that I hated being with them, but I hated the stigma associated with being in the "slow" class. After spending time in the class, however, I observed that most of the so-called slow students were neither dumb nor slow learners, they were Black. That should have occurred to me when I first entered the classroom, but I overlooked it. For some reason, I just accepted the number of Black students as normal, especially since I was constantly reminded of my supposedly inferior intelligence by White teachers and authority figures. Unconsciously and sometimes consciously, I felt that White students were actually smarter than Black students anyway, so I had no reason to question why so many Blacks students were in the slow classes or special education classes.

After about three weeks in Special Ed, I mustered up enough nerve to tell my mother that I was in special education and that I was retarded. At first my mother laughed at me thinking that I was just telling one of my usual jokes. When I started crying, she realized that I was telling the truth and became irate at me and my counselor. "Why didn't you tell me?" she asked. I explained that I was too embarrassed, and I reminded her about her testimony about me being retarded. She said, "Girl, ain't nothing wrong with you. You may act retarded, but you not." If I would have not been so relieved, her comments would have hurt me deeply. But my mother said I wasn't retarded, and I knew that she should know since I was her child.

The next morning, we went to the principal's office and explained the horrendous mistake that was made. The principal didn't seem to care, and it was obvious to me that he hated Black people. He nonchalantly called the counselor in and asked her about the situation. My mother was insulted because she had just recounted the entire incident to the principal, but I knew that my Black mother's word was not good enough for him. The counselor said that I had scored low on the placement tests; however, she agreed to review my case. My mother demanded a review on the spot, and the counselor reluctantly retrieved my test scores. With my mother by her side, the counselors compared my test scores with the national averages; and guess what, I scored three grades ahead in English, language, and history. I scored two grades ahead in math and one grade ahead in science. The counselor turned red realizing that she screwed up my results. She apologized like nothing significant happened, and she cautioned my mother against placing me in a regular classroom despite my test scores. She felt that a regular classroom environment would be too overwhelming for me. In other words she was saying, "I don't care what the test results say, your daughter is still a dumb nigger."

The counselor offered no explanation for the mix up. She didn't even offer an apology, an excuse, or anything. The bigoted woman did not even offer to make amends and place me into a regular classroom. She just sat and stared at my mother, and her callous demeanor revealed her contempt for having darkies challenge and correct her. It was obvious that she didn't give a damn about me. So she made a mistake that could have potentially affected a child's education for life, so what! She was not concerned the least bit.

The principal maintained his unconcerned attitude throughout the meeting. He offered no words of support for me, and he didn't try to support the counselor. It was obvious that he had better things to do than to worry about a Black student who was unfairly placed in special education. Without offering any comforting words to me or my mother, he called his secretary into his office and ordered her to place me in into Mr. Such-and-such's class. No, he didn't escort me and my mother to my new class, he just wrote my new teacher a note and mumbled directions to my new classroom.

With a month and a half left in the school year, I entered into another classroom. Making friends was the least of my worries because I just wanted to successfully complete all of my homework and classroom assignments. I would sometimes do additional homework and memorize words in the dictionary just to prove to myself that I wasn't stupid, retarded, or dumb. Being placed in Special Ed. had somewhat destroyed the little confidence I had in my ability to learn. I constantly questioned and quizzed myself to ensure that my memory worked. Irrespective of what anybody said, I studied because I still believed that retardation was right around the corner. I vowed to myself that I would never be placed in Special Ed. again, and I promised myself to become an exceptional student. I had to because I could never risk suffering such humiliation again. It was up to me to excel at school, just God and me.

Now I wonder how many of the other Black children in the Special Ed. class were misplaced or misdiagnosed. If I was a betting woman, I would say the majority. And if their parents never removed them from special education in order for them to receive adequate instruction, stimulation, and attention, they would have developed into *true* special education students. They would have fallen behind year after year. I almost feel like it was a conspiracy to put as many Black children in Special Ed. as possible—teach them nothing, allow them to be unruly, allow them to accept being nonproductive, allow them to accept being underachievers so Whites could say, "See, I told you *they* were intellectually inferior."

Racism had almost defeated me again, and I had almost become a victim to one of the oldest plots in history—make people hate and doubt themselves, and then control them. This plan worked effectively during the time of Black slavery and was one of the primary reasons why slaveholding Whites were able to control and dominate Blacks. The slaveholders were able to break the slaves' spirit and confidence, thereby, convincing the slaves that they were unable to survive without the mental, emotional, and physical comforts of "Massa."

My experience in Special Ed. also taught me not to judge people who are physically challenged or who are challenged in ways that I am not. Even though some of the students were physically challenged, they were intelligent human beings who were also victimized by prejudice and stereotypes. I am sure that many teachers felt that the physically challenged students were intellectually inferior, just like they felt that Black students were intellectually inferior. I learned an important lesson—don't form judgments on outward appearances alone—looks are deceiving, ignorance is powerful, and apathy is deadly.

From then on, I knew I had to count on me to make my own judgments about people regardless of the constant bombardment that I received from the media. It was up to me to see people just as people and not the caricatures that newspapers, researchers, and authority figures made them out to be.

I also knew I had to prove that I wasn't an underachiever, and so I accepted the responsibility to learn on my own and by myself. I took action. I studied, I read, and I discussed. I promised myself that my intellectual ability would never be questioned. I was capable of learning, and I knew that I could depend on me, just God and me.

CHAPTER 7

# Low Expectations = Low Performance

OUR STAY IN Brentwood, Missouri was short-lived due to my father's new pastoral assignment to two small churches in the boondocks. One church, Smith Chapel United Methodist, was located in Sikeston, Missouri, which is about 150 miles south of St. Louis. The smaller church, First United Methodist, was located in Hayti, Missouri, which is about 190 miles south of St. Louis and fifty-three miles from Sikeston. It was truly a difficult arrangement for my father and for the church members of both church congregations because they both wanted a full-time minister, yet they could not afford to support one by themselves.

To accommodate both churches, my father alternated preaching and visiting the churches on separate Sundays. The first and third Sundays, we attended Smith Chapel; and on second and fourth Sundays, we attended First United. My family preferred to attend Smith Chapel because the one-hour commute to Hayti was unbearable. By the time we arrived in Hayti, we were in no mood for worshipping God. You see, our car could not comfortably accommodate three growing children in the back seat and two adults and one infant in the front seat. As a result, we argued, complained, and fought all the way there and back. Treating each other with the love of the Lord was not a priority. Driving in a beat-up car to preach to a handful of people would even test the patience of Jesus.

We moved to Sikeston since Smith Chapel had a parsonage across the street. It was a two-bedroom, one-bathroom house on Young Street. The house had neither central heating nor air-conditioning, which made it miserable in the summer and winter months. In the summer, we were forced to open the windows and use fans for ventilation. Since most of the screens were old, we had to contend with mosquitoes, flies, and other insects entering the house at will. In the winter, we had to sleep in the living room by a pot-bellied furnace if we wanted to stay warm. I didn't feel deprived, however, because everybody else in the community had the same living conditions.

Like I said, I didn't mind the living conditions after I adjusted. But I must admit, that at first, I resented living in a small house and in Sikeston. I had grown accustomed to living in a predominately White, middle-class, four-bedroom townhouse with a few amenities like central air-conditioning and heating. We were by no means middle-class, and I didn't particularly enjoy living alongside all-White people, but my parents worked hard to ensure that we lived in safe neighborhoods since their schedules didn't allow them to spend a lot of time at home. But like I mentioned earlier, I adjusted.

The church members at Smith Chapel were the friendliest people that I had ever met. When we arrived, we were greeted with large pies, cakes, fried chicken, and pretty much any soul-food dish that you can imagine. I was in food heaven. One deacon, Mr. Motton, agreed to add a bedroom on the house to make it more comfortable for our large family. The people were very hospitable and truly exemplified the word "Christian."

Sikeston was a racially divided town and the railroad tracks served as the unofficial, but official boundary between White City and Chocolate City. Both cities had their own set of projects that were reserved for low-income families. Both cities had their own grocery stores, beauty shops, churches, etc., which made racial mixing unnecessary or discouraged. If you talked to Blacks, the majority would say that racial mixing except at school was *unnecessary*. However, if you talked to the majority of Whites, the majority would overtly say or subtly imply that racial mixing was *discouraged*. You see, everything depended upon who you talked to.

Of course, our family lived in Chocolate City behind the railroad tracks, but we shopped and did our laundry in White City. My mother insisted that we had good food to eat, which meant that we had to go to the other side of town to get the freshest meat and fresh vegetables. The stores on the Black side of town carried a limited variety of foods and carried more pork than anything else. They sold every part of the pig imaginable. They sold chitterlings, hog jowls, pig ears, pig tails, pig snout, pig feet, and other pig parts that I wasn't familiar with. They sold some hamburger and chicken but it wasn't high quality. It always looked a day old or smelled a little foul. The stores in the Black community always had stacks of hotdogs and bologna—fatty, unhealthy foods—and seldom sold any type of fish.

Stores in the Black community also carried more varieties of beers, wines, and cigarettes than I had ever seen in my life. They had names like Malt Duck, Bull, and other brands that I had only seen advertised on street signs and on local billboards. Cigarettes were not kept behind the counter either, and children were allowed to purchase them. I thought it was cool at the time, but now I realize how destructive it was to have cigarettes and beer readily available to children and young adults.

Since my father had one more year to complete his Master's degree, he lived in St. Louis with my Grandma Mildred. On Fridays he would take the Greyhound bus to Sikeston, visit with us on Saturday, preach at one of his churches on Sunday morning, and return to St. Louis on Sunday night. His schedule was almost unbearable, but he never let on to us that it was taking a toll on his studies, job, health, or his marriage to my mother. To my brother, sisters, and me, everything was fine.

Even though I missed my father dearly, I wasn't too upset about not having a father in the house because the majority of my friends didn't live with their fathers either. Some didn't even know who their fathers were, so I felt lucky that Daddy spent time with us even for brief periods. My father's absence also gave me and my sister more freedom because my mother allowed us to run the streets. I am sure she wanted to exercise more control over our lives, but she worked in a hospital in Cape Giradue, which was thirty miles away, because there were few well-paying nursing jobs nearby. Since she needed to make the most money she could to help support us and help pay for my father's tuition, she accepted a position thirty miles away and was forced to rely on us to take care of ourselves. Boy, I really enjoyed the freedom, and I never abused it because I understood that my mother had no other choice. Just seeing both of my parents working and grinding so hard made me honor their rules. I was proud of them even though I did not know how to show or express it.

The town of Sikeston had three elementary schools, one middle school, one junior high school, and one senior high school all located on the White side of town. Most students in the Black community were bussed from

Chocolate City to White City to attend school. I felt that it was unfair that there were few schools located in our side of town, but few Blacks shared my frustration. Since I was not raised in Sikeston, I had a different mentality and perspective regarding fairness. And since we had just moved to the community, I did not have an opportunity to inculcate or imbibe the town's values, norms, or ways of life. To me, it felt unfair that we were being bussed or shipped to what felt like the other side of creation to attend school. And I didn't understand why only the Blacks kids had to be inconvenienced. Why did the Black people have to get up early to catch a bus? Why did we have to wait outside in the cold until the bus came? I am sure White students had to catch buses to attend school also, but I did not know that at the time. All I saw and experienced was inequity, which did not sit well with my constant and pervasive feelings of being "less than." As I shared earlier, I expected less of everything. However, receiving less started to anger me. My spirit was beginning to have a harder time digesting and accepting my second-class designation. Second-class status started to suck!

My father's job at Project Equality raised my awareness about race and race relations, and I had become hypersensitive and hyper-vigilant about injustice. I witnessed racism and experienced racism despite not being able to totally articulate the concept of racism. But despite my inability to explain racism and give a theoretical overview of what prejudice is, I could easily identify it. I knew what it meant in my soul. From a child, I was taught and drilled on how to respond to and behave around White people. I saw my parents and grandparents model "appropriate" White-people behavior; so I was totally aware, informed, and prepared to deal with prejudice. And even though I could not accurately explain what bias was, I knew how it manifested. I felt what it was. And I was indirectly taught how to coexist with it and to function in the midst of it. But as I matured and my awareness of racial disparities and inequalities grew, I became increasingly angry, frustrated, and defeated. As I got older, I inherently knew that there were systems in place that supported and ensured the racial divide. I could not identify or pinpoint the systems; however, I could mentally detect that some systems or forces were operating to maintain the racial status quo. The old adage that states that "ignorance is bliss" is true. The more I understood, the more uncomfortable, annoyed, and bitter I became.

The middle school classes were divided into four levels: Special Education Regular, Major, and Maximum. The kids in Special Education were defined as slow learners or unofficially considered to be underachievers. Unlike my previous experience, the special education classrooms had both Black and White students equally represented, so I did not get the feeling that the Blacks students were being unfairly tracked. The Regular classrooms were for students of low to average intelligence, and the majority of students in Regular were Blacks. Since I was new to the school and the school system, I was immediately placed in Regular classes. I was not tested to determine my academic ability or to assess my academic potential. I was Black, and so to the school officials, I was properly placed in my appropriate educational category.

The Major classes was reserved for students who were considered to have average to above-average intelligence, and who were considered disciplined. "Disciplined" was never defined so I had no idea what that category officially meant. But since ninety percent of the students enrolled in Major classes were White, I assumed that "disciplined" was a buzz word to limit Black enrollment. To me, it was the way that the school system ensured that Black students would not have the same challenging curriculum as the White students. I couldn't articulate it then, but I felt that in some way the school system was perpetuating the separate-but-equal philosophy. I am not sure if the education provided in Regular was subpar, I just knew that the academic rigor and expectations in Major were significantly greater. The books were different and the assignments were different. And I wondered if the students inRegular class would really have an opportunity to catch up with the more advanced students. I felt that the students in Regular started from behind and would always academically be behind the other students. It was not fair to me, but it also felt unfair to me that the Blacks student and parents did not protest this "levelism."

Maximum classes were reserved for the intellectually elite, gifted students. To my knowledge, there was only one Black enrolled in Maximum classes, and he acted and associated only with Whites. It was rumored that his parents were teachers in the school district, so we just assumed that his intelligence was hereditary. Nobody cared that he associated with Whites only either because he was a nerdy, weird-looking guy who we referred to as the "Oreo kid."

After my unfortunate placement in special education in Brentwood, my mother visited Sikeston Middle School two weeks after school started to ensure that I was properly placed in academically-challenging classes. She was informed by the principal that my sister and I were placed in Regular classes. The principal told her that we didn't need to take any tests to determine our grade level because he was *sure* that Regular level would *suit* us fine. My mother told the principal that we were smart children and demanded all Maximum classes for us. I was proud that my mother had so much confidence in my ability to learn; however, I was not confident about taking Maximum classes. My unfortunate placement in special education had affected my self-esteem, and I wasn't totally sure that I could keep up with the gifted students. My mother assured me that I could. I didn't believe her, but I promised her that I would try. Also, I vowed that I was not going to look like a fool in front of the White kids.

After the conference, I was given a new class schedule, and off to class I went. The first class I entered was English. Since I was entering the class late, I had to approach the teacher's desk to get her signature. To say that my teacher and new classmates were surprised to see me would be a gross understatement. From their stares, you would have thought that I was an alien from outer space, a Martian or something. The students' eyes followed me to the teacher's desk, and their glares were so intense that I felt naked. After my teacher regained her composure, she told me to take a seat. Only the back seats were vacant because the students in Maximum class were excited about learning and competed to seat in the front row. Sitting in the back for me was comfortable because that's all I knew. It was obvious too that the White kids didn't want to sit next to me anyway; so I felt relieved to be at the back by myself, free of them as well.

The students in Regular, Major, and Maximum had different lunch schedules, so I didn't see any of my Black friends until gym class. I happily told them about my transfer to Maximum classes in expectation of receiving their congratulations and support. At first, they said nothing and just stared at me and then at each other. They asked me why I transferred out of Regular. I informed my friends that I transferred because my mother thought that I was too smart for Regular. Then I said, "Maximum isn't really that hard either." After I said that, I knew I had invited trouble. I didn't mean to say something so stupid or insensitive. I wasn't thinking. If I had been thinking, I would have understood that my comment would make me public enemy number one. Well, my friends just looked at me with disdain and said, “You don’t have to brag about it. We don’t care anyway, and you will have to do a lot of homework too. You will see. You are going to wish that you stayed in with us.”

Even though I should have used better discretion, I was stunned by the Black students’ continued reaction to my statement. The word got around that I was bragging and belittling other students. I was shocked because I only made one comment, and I really did not mean any harm by my statements. I was merely stating the truth. The class lessons were demanding but manageable. From then on, I never told anyone else that I was in Maximum classes, but the word got around anyway. So on the bus, I was constantly bombarded with questions about anything and everything. I wanted to yell, “I am in Maximum classes, but I am not an encyclopedia.” And heaven forbid if I answered a question incorrectly. I would have to hear, “You ain’t that smart,” “I thought you knew everything,” “And you think you better than us, don’t you?” It got to the point that I feared helping people with their homework too. If they received a good grade, they loved me. If they received a C or below, my life or nose was threatened. It was definitely a lose-lose situation.

After about two months in Maximum, the White students slowly started accepting my presence in the gifted class. I still had to work by myself on group projects because nobody ever wanted to work with me, and the teacher never encouraged them to either. I had to work hard to compete. Luckily, I had developed an amazing memory during the summer and could sometimes perfectly recall passages that I read, science formulas that I had seen, etc. To this day, I still remember that the scientific formula for sugar is $C_6H_{12}0_6$ and NaCl for salt. Being unfairly placed in Special Ed. resulted in one benefit: it encouraged me to develop my memory, which became a resource for me that I could always rely on in stressful academic situations.

On my first report card, I think I received two As and four Bs. I could have done better, but I was too busy running the streets with my friends and enjoying my new freedom. Since I had developed a good memory, I seldom studied for tests. I really only had to apply myself in math class because I actually had to understand how to work the problems. The other classes were not a breeze but manageable.

After we received our report cards, the students in Maximum classes compared their grades. They bragged to each other and challenged each other for the next semester. I bragged also because I felt proud that I did as well as or better than they did in some subjects. Their reactions varied. Some White students were amazed that I was as smart as they were, some didn't believe me and wanted to see my report card, and others felt threatened and glared at me. I knew the students that felt threatened did not approve of my achievements and were going to retaliate somehow, but I wasn't sure how.

I lied to the Black students and told them that I received all Cs. I felt guilty about lying, but I had to live in the Black community, and I didn't want to make enemies. I remembered the reactions that I received when I told people about my transfer to Maximum and I didn't want to suffer anymore abuse. After revealing my mediocre performance, I instantly had friends again. People even supported me and told me that I could always come back to Regular. Their joyous reaction to my lies demonstrated that they were not my friends. From then on, I vowed to never reveal my grades again. I also vowed to get all As the next semester to really show them and myself how smart I was. Again I was on a mission.

To accomplish my mission, I increased my study time to four hours a night. Even if I didn't have assigned homework, I read ahead in my textbooks and checked out books on any subjects that we discussed in the classroom. If I didn't understand certain concepts, I scheduled tutoring time with my teachers. I even asked the other students in my classes for assistance. I never left a stone unturned if it would assist me with attaining my educational goals. Furthermore, I limited my interaction with people whose jealously and ill-will hindered my success.

As a result of my tenacity, my grades improved dramatically. My enthusiasm was tempered, however, by the taunts that I received from jealous White students. They would call me Kunta Kente and Kizzy, characters from the widely-acclaimed TV series, *Roots*. *Roots* was an inspirational show in the '70s that depicted the hardships of slavery, and so I wasn't upset about the name calling at first. When the students realized that I was not affected by those names, they added adjectives like Nigger Girl Kizzy. Some students would even recount the episode of *Kunta Kente* being whipped for not accepting the name given to him by his new slave master. I tried to ignore their comments, but I became suspicious of their motives. I didn't know if they were trying to imply that they were going to inflict bodily harm on me, or if they were trying to affect me emotionally by making light of a very serious situation. Despite their antics, my resolve to kick their butts academically remained.

I confided in a few Black students, whom I thought were my friends, about the harassment that I received. Most felt that I brought the situation on myself by wanting to be with *them* instead of being in Regular classes. I was still puzzled by their reactions to my placement in Maximum, especially since it had been almost four months since my transfer. Suffice it to say, I received no support or empathy from the majority of Black students. At times, I felt that they were actually pleased by the racist comments and harassment that I received. I believed they enjoyed the White students teaching me a lesson.

After about one month of taunts, my concentration was affected. I became paranoid and feared going into the bathroom by myself, walking to gym or to the music room by myself, etc. I became overly cautious about my student locker because I feared that some students wanted to sabotage my assignments and projects. I always panicked when we had to exchange and grade each other's papers in class. Many times, my words or answers were changed which prevented me from getting As. I knew my teachers were aware of what was happening, and I honestly felt that some teachers condoned the students' behavior. When one student unfairly changed four answers on a pop quiz, I told my mother what was happening. I told her that students were harassing me and changing answers on my tests to lower my test scores. She immediately met with my principal, who denied that students were capable of such behavior. He practically called me a liar and stated that if I had trouble doing the work, he would gladly transfer me to another class. His reaction cut me like a knife. I decided then that I had to depend on me to deal with my unconcerned teachers that sanctioned the students' behavior as well as the students that made my life a living hell.

Unfortunately the next week, I snapped. I was in the bathroom combing my hair when a group of White girls entered and said, "Look at Kizzy combing her nappy hair." That phrase didn't faze me because my hair was nappy. Then one of the girls snatched the comb out of my hand. I panicked because I knew that I couldn't beat up six girls; I was outnumbered. But

I also knew that I would not be bullied. I understood that I had to do something drastic or I could get hurt. I knew I had to do something that would shock them to prevent them from hurting me.

Like a wounded animal, I jumped on the girl who snatched my comb and rammed her head into a toilet commode. From then on, anger consumed me. All of the pent up anger from the school year energized me, and I felt physically strong as if I were Samson or the Incredible Hulk. I was enraged and scared at the same time. I held the girl's head under the water hoping to drown her. At that very moment, I wanted to kill the girl, and I honestly enjoyed the fear that I saw in the other girls' eyes. I wanted to yell, "Now you know how I feel. Now you see what's it is like to feel terrified! Now you have a glimpse into my daily life at this freakin' school!" Then something came over me, and I released the girl's head. She was turning blue and was gasping for air and crying hysterically. In that moment, I didn't care. I had no compassion or empathy for her. Why should I? No one had shown any compassion for me? I was tired of being harassed and intimidated. And I knew that nobody else would bother me after that incident. I knew I was going to get in trouble and possibly be expelled from school, but I wasn't concerned. However, the more I thought about what I had done, the more nervous I became. I couldn't believe that I almost killed somebody, and it shocked me that getting revenge didn't feel so bad. Without getting permission, I just left school and cried as I walked home. "Oh God," I cried, "what have I done?" Guilt completely overwhelmed me despite my attempts to rationalize what I had done. I feared the wrath of God too because I knew that murder was one of the Ten Commandments—an unpardonable sin. I also feared the wrath of my parents, who would be totally convinced that I had lost my last piece of good sense.

I didn't immediately tell anybody what happened, but a few people knew that something serious had occurred because of my unusual behavior. I talked rapidly and my thoughts were scattered. I bit my fingernails and twisted my hair. My behavior was so uncharacteristic that one adult friend, Bev, asked me if some children beat me up on the bus. I wanted to tell her what happened, but I thought that playing twenty questions with her with would minimize the impact of what I did. She finally asked me if I needed to defend myself at school. I said yes, but I didn't explain why. I started crying hysterically and told her that God was going to punish me because I tried to kill somebody. My comments and reactions alarmed her. Patiently and tactfully, she asked me how I tried to kill somebody. I told her that I tried to drown a girl in the toilet commode. I kept apologizing and pleaded for her to pray for me. Bev waited calmly while I regained my composure and then tried to comfort me by explaining that I had to defend myself. Her words temporarily consoled me, and I fell asleep in her arms.

The following day, I went to school ready to confess to the crime that I committed, but the girl had not revealed what I had done. I attempted to act normal in class, but I jumped every time somebody entered the classroom. I was so rattled with guilt that I was convinced the principal or the police were going to pull me out of class and haul me off to jail. But nothing happened. I waited and waited.

From the White students' reactions, I knew they were aware of what occurred in the bathroom. Nobody had the guts to ask me directly, but I am sure they knew. When they thought that I wasn't looking, they stared at me or exchanged glances with their friends. After a while, I realized that they were afraid of me. Maybe they thought that I would attack them too. I prayed to God for strength and remained calm for most of the day.

The second day after the bathroom incident, I was called into the principal's office. Lucky for me I had one day to gather my thoughts and determine how I would protest if I was expelled. As I walked in the principal's office, I immediately felt outnumbered because the girl was there with her parents. I wanted to call my mother, but she had already left for work. For some reason, I felt relaxed and composed. The principal motioned for me to have a seat, and I sat down. I sat erect to show that I wasn't scared of them, and my calm demeanor unnerved the principal.

The principal requested to hear my version of what happened in the bathroom. I explained what happened slowly and deliberately. I told him that I had been constantly harassed by the students in my classes for the last five months. I explained that yesterday I was combing my hair in the bathroom when the girl called me Kizzy and said that my hair was nappy. I told him that I felt threatened because there were six girls making fun of me, and I thought that they were going to hurt me. I pointed to the girl and said that she snatched my comb out of my hand. I told him that I became so angry, I put her head in the toilet. I denied trying to hurt the girl, but I told him that I felt that I had to do something extreme so the other girls wouldn't gang up on me.

At least the girl agreed with my version of the story and didn't lie about snatching my comb. Her confession and her parent's reaction to her admission perplexed me. They did not excuse or condone her behavior. They did not treat me with contempt or disregard my account of what happened. Something about these White people were different; they behaved in a way that felt as if they wanted to be fair. I wondered to myself if these were a new type of White people. Maybe they were Northerners or something. I wanted, really needed, to know if other White people like them existed. I had met one who worked with my dad, but that was it. If there were more White people like her parents, I wanted to meet them and beg them to train/teach my teachers how to behave so my life would not be so hard in school.

The principal gave me some lecture about fighting, but I tuned him out. I didn't hear a word he said until he said that I had a three-day suspension. I tried not to show my relief in my eyes because I thought my punishment would be expulsion. He gave me a note for my mother to sign and told me to leave the school's premises. I followed his orders and walked three miles home.

On the way home, I replayed the incident over in my mind. What made me snap? Am I a bad person or just mean? Am I going to hell? I pondered these questions hoping to understand why I acted so violently. I knew I had to protect myself, but was there another way to handle the situation? By the time I arrived home, I still had no answers for my behavior; however, I felt peaceful. I had experienced a different brand of White people, and my punishment wasn't too severe. God was good!

Two weeks after the incident, I still felt embarrassed by my actions, but I felt proud how I handled the situation in the bathroom and the conference with the girl's parents. I realized that years of racist comments and experiences had created a volcano, and snatching my comb made me erupt. Now that I realized that my emotional wounds never had an opportunity to heal, I promised myself to monitor my behavior. I didn't want my anger to control me, nor did I want to become the stereotypical violent Black youth which was exactly what Whites expected. Again I had to depend on me to direct my life in a way that preserved my self-respect and dignity.

I also had to depend on me to continue excelling in school despite the ridicule that I endured from White students and the lack of support I received from Black students, who desperately wanted me to fail. I became more determined to achieve my goals even if it meant losing or alienating friends and infuriating my enemies. If I wanted success, I had to depend on me. Just God and me!

After the bathroom incident, I became an outcast in my classes. The few people who talked to me did so reluctantly. Their discomfort showed by their inability to speak in full sentences or phrases to me when I initiated a discussion. My classmates seldom said hi to me, and when they did, they had difficulty looking me in the eyes. I wanted to yell, "I'm not a violent animal, and I will not hurt you." Even if I did make that announcement, it would not have helped because people were unnerved by what I did. To tell the truth, I would have not wanted to be friends with a person who I felt was capable of murder either, so I didn't take their snubs personally. I understood that the Whites did not and could not appreciate the constant fear and angst I suffered in the classrooms, lunchrooms, hallways, bathrooms, and gym. They could not relate, so if being thought to be a murderer prevented future attacks, I was happy. I did not want to fight, and God knows, I did not want to get jumped.

My teachers' reactions on the other hand concerned me. They never mentioned what happened in the bathroom either, but I knew they had heard some exaggerated account of what occurred. Immediately following the incident, two teachers canceled my tutoring time without any explanations. When I pressed them for explanations, it was apparent they had no excuses. I assumed they didn't feel safe with me. And, I didn't know what to do either to reassure them because I never had grown-ups scared of me before. I just tried my best to explain to them that I needed and appreciated their help because I wanted to maintain my grades. I felt like crying as I realized that nothing I said was going to change their minds, but I didn't. I knew there was nothing I could do to make them feel comfortable or safe with me. But most of all, I knew it was up to me to find another person willing to help me with my math and English projects.

After two teacher assistants refused to or "didn't have time" to tutor me, I felt that something larger was happening. I felt as though I was being punished, being taught a lesson for hurting a White girl, or for being violent. I wasn't sure which. I wanted to confront my teachers and demand to know why they were responding to me this way, but I couldn't. Any interaction would have been perceived as aggression. Even though I was only in the sixth grade, I wasn't a fool. Thanks to racism, I was wise beyond my years when it came to race relations.

With little assistance, I was only able to earn a B in math. I wasn't satisfied with my grade because I knew with some extra help I could have earned an A. Teachers refusing to help me made me resent them, and I started having dreams about hurting them. When I shared my dreams with my mother, she was horrified by their sadistic nature. What alarmed her most was when I talked about punching my teacher in the face in a calm and deliberate voice. My mother never condemned me for my dreams, but her concerned looks told me she was worried about me. There was no explanation that I could provide either for my horrific dreams. I just knew that I felt powerless at school, and my dreams were the only place where I won, where I had the power.

Luckily, my mother was able to help me with my English project because she had a lot of experience doing term papers. To me, researching and writing a term paper was overwhelming. All the Maximum classes had to complete one term paper before entering seventh grade, so I knew I had to complete one also. We got to choose a subject, but we had to follow the research and structure guidelines given to us by our teacher. I appreciated the guidelines too because it gave me direction when I felt lost at the library or anxious about the actual writing of the paper.

Before we actually started writing our papers, we had to get our subjects and outlines approved. I knew that my English teacher would scrutinize my paper more harshly than the other students because I chose to write about Martin Luther King. So when my father came home for the weekend, we refined my contact statement, outline, and listed my research sources. My father also typed the entire thing for me, and my mother bought me a clear folder to put my information in. Boy, I couldn't wait until Monday to see my teacher's face.

On Monday, I walked into English class with a smile on my face and pep in my step. I turned in my clear folder with my term paper information in it and walked to my seat. My teacher looked at my typed submission and glared at me. I knew that I had won. I knew that my outline was so thorough that she had to give me an A and approve my topic. I tried not to reveal the "gotcha" look on my face, but I was too proud of my accomplishment, and I felt honored my parents helped me to outsmart my teacher. Needless to say, I received an A on my first term paper, and I felt like me and Martin Luther King had truly overcome. I had won. Excellence had prevailed.

The school year ended soon after I turned in my paper. I think I received three Bs and four As on my final report card. I knew that I could have done better with tutoring, but it wasn't available. I had to depend on me. Luckily, I could also depend on my parents to help achieve my goal of being an excellent, superior student. I was ecstatic. I had my parents, God, and me. But mainly, God and me.

Despite my good grades and despite always being a well-mattered student, I learned that any attempt to physically protect myself intimidated and angered Whites. Honestly, I could not and still cannot understand their audacity. I endured the racial slurs, the teachers' indifference, racist lesson plans, the collusion of conniving students, and administrative injustices, and I was the student who was rumored to have acted inappropriately? Even though my personal safety was threatened and I had a legitimate reason to defend myself, I was the poorly behaved child? The problem was that Blacks defending themselves against White's injustice was unexpected, unacceptable, and unnerving. And some White students and teachers challenging their own racist behavior was unheard of. So, to them, I must have fit the widely-held stereotype about Black people, a stereotype that was deeply embedded in revisionist history and in the psyches of some White people. I was unruly, animalistic, violent, and unpredictable. But the truth was that their racism and bigotry were equally as violent; it was an emotional attack on my spirit and my personhood. Their racist attitudes were intractable, and their responses to me were capricious. I never knew what type of hurt to expect, but I knew to expect hurt. So if staying alive and protecting myself meant that I had proven a stereotype, I am grateful that I could depend on God and me, but mostly God and just a little bit of me.

## CHAPTER 8

# Uncontained Poison

THE SUMMER PROVIDED the breaks I needed—a break from the pressures of school, a break from the isolation I felt in the classroom, a break from White teachers and students who resented my academic excellence, and a break from the torment I received from Black students about being in Maximum classes. Nothing special was planned for the summer due to my parent's financial situation. Every extra dime went to my father's tuition at Eden Seminary or my mother's tuition at South East Missouri State. Working full-time jobs and attending school left little time for my parents to be with us, and I desperately missed having them around fully energized and alert. So many times when we spent time with my parents, they were physically and mentally exhausted, which left them little energy to deal with four children. We missed them at first, but by the middle of the summer, we were accustomed to having no one around to advise and guide us. Consequently, my brother and sister started hanging with the wrong crowd. I stayed home with my three-year-old sister and became a soap opera junkie.

After dressing myself and my sister, I would spend numerous hours watching *The Young and Restless, Search for Tomorrow,* and *As the World Turns*. The more I watched, the more fascinated I became. I would daydream about wearing beautiful clothes, having flowing long hair, and living in a beautiful home. My daily viewing of soaps was my escape from my mundane life of watching over my little sister, living in a small home, and owning few clothes. It was what I wanted to become. Sadly, I started having dreams about being in a soap opera as a White woman with blonde hair. I didn't realize that White women were gradually becoming my definition of beauty, success, and power; but luckily, my father was the first to notice this change because I never had anything positive to say about Black entertainers. I always said that White entertainers were more beautiful, could sing better, could dance better, and do everything else better than Black entertainers. I feel so fortunate that my father made me aware of the poison—the images and thoughts of White superiority—that I was feeding my mind.

Soon the summer was over and school began. I still had to attend Sikeston Middle School, so I started preparing myself for another long and eventful school year. Again I was enrolled in all Maximum classes, but luckily my friends started accepting that I was in Max and didn't bother me. They still made comments behind my back, but most of the crude remarks to my face ceased. During the summer, I also developed close relationships with two girls, Arlene and Patricia, and just having them around made me feel more included in the Black school community than the year before.

What I remember most about seventh grade is my history class. My history class was taught by a short man with a pointy nose, who wore pointed toe boots called "roach killers". Even though he was five feet four, he strutted around in class as if he were eight feet tall. He was excited about American history and excited the students as well. He would have been considered a great teacher if he was able to teach objectively without interjecting his racist views and comments about Native Americans and Black Americans.

I clearly recall a discussion about the American Manifest Destiny. I remember him saying, "If it hadn't been for the White man, America wouldn't be what it is today." Starting class with such a statement alarmed me, and my prejudice antenna went up. I didn't say anything at the time because I didn't know this teacher, and I didn't want to upset him so early in the school year.

For the next couple of weeks he discussed Manifest Destiny and how the White men saved and civilized the wild "Injuns." He never pronounced the word Indian correctly, and every time he said Injuns, it cut me like a knife. He made the word Indian sound dirty, degrading, and disgusting. Even a four-letter word was less abrasive to the ear. I tried not to hear him when he said Injuns, but I couldn't help it. Minutes after he would say the word Injun, the word would reverberate in my ears.

In addition, he always made negative comments about Indians. He called them savages, killers, and warriors. I can't remember him ever using a positive adjective to describe America's indigenous people. Never! He talked about their religion with so much disdain that it offended me, even though I was ignorant about their religious customs and beliefs. I was truly hurt and felt wounded not only because my great grandmother was a Cherokee Indian but because my classmates laughed at his racist comments. Some actually thought that his degrading remarks were funny and entertaining. Or if they did not agree with him, they laughed to conceal their discomfort. But to me, laughing, regardless of the reason, felt painful. The more the students laughed, the angrier I became. I wanted to yell and chastise them for laughing at such a serious matter. But I was outnumbered, and I knew that the teacher wouldn't come to my rescue if the students started verbally abusing me. I felt powerless, worthless, and severely victimized.

The last straw was when my teacher started talking about how lazy the Indians were. He explained how Indians were reluctant to "help the settlers," but I knew he meant that the indigenous people would not willingly submit to slavery. He explained that the settlers, to me it was a code word for White men, had no other alternative but to "place them on reservations to be cared for." Yikes! I wanted to yell, "Liar," but I was scared. My teacher also gave the impression that Indians were physically inferior because they couldn't withstand the White man's diseases. What the teacher did not explain was that the native people had never been exposed to the *same* diseases. As a result, they had not built up immunity to the diseases that were common to the White settlers. But he did not offer that explanation. No additional information or clarification was provided to put the historical accounts in context. No admissions or any suggestions that germs were secretly given to the Indians that decimated their families. Nothing! Everything he said was twisted; it had a kernel of truth that was lost in a sea of lies and omissions. Any information that highlighted any of the atrocities inflicted by the White settlers were absent from his educational tirades.

Some White students felt that his racist lectures were extremely amusing and laughed uncontrollably. Or they laughed out of discomfort. Who knows? What hurt most was seeing the "Oreo Kid," the Black student who acted White, laughing hysterically with the group. What a fool! He didn't even realize that the next group that would be the focus of laughter would be us—Blacks. I left class because I couldn't stomach the teacher's smirking face or the red faces of my laughing classmates. I ran to the locker room and cried. I cried about the atrocities done to the Indians at the hands of the White man and about the atrocities that I knew had been inflicted on Blacks. I mourned and grieved because I felt that some of my classmates had the same vicious spirits that some White settlers had back then. In my spirit, I felt that nothing really had changed since the 1500s. To me, inaccurate history books and negative portrayals on TV had made degrading and belittling non-Whites easy and acceptable. There was little thought to the impact that historically inaccurate Western movies and Tarzan-like movies had on the psyches of non-white kids. I felt that nobody questioned if the movies or the inaccuracies hurt and wounded us physically, emotionally, and spiritually.

My teacher's glorification of slavery was just as appalling as his opinion of Native Americans. He didn't say that Africans were savages or warriors, he referred to them as pagans. When he discussed the slave trade, he constantly referred to Africans as commodities that were traded for sugar and cotton. He never attributed human qualities to the "commodities" either; they were just a medium of exchange, a form of money, an indication of wealth, a means to power. He explained that the "commodities" were transported in ships, not crowded and cramped in unsanitary boats. He constantly harped about the massive expense associated with the slave trade. To me, it appeared that he wanted to portray how White men sacrificed profits to clothe and fed their human chattel. He tried his best to paint the White traders as benevolent businessmen.

My history teacher's most abhorrent thesis was his explanation about how Africans "encouraged" slavery by their own willingness to sell other Africans to White traders. I knew that some African tribes sold their prisoners of war and their enemies to White settlers, but Africans didn't initiate the idea of the type of slavery that the White settlers practiced. It was my understanding at that time that Whites settlers were initially welcomed by the Africans. I knew that Africans accepted White traders and showed them their villages and the riches of the African continent. However, after being exposed to riches of White men, some Africans sold out their African brothers for wealth, luxury, and respect in their villages. I'm sorry to say that some Blacks continue this practice today. In essence, my history teacher was attempting to absolve the White students of any guilt for the slave trade by emphasizing that the Africans—the victims—initiated, accepted, endorsed, participated, and organized one of the most inhuman institutions in the history of the United States.

When discussing the trading process of slaves, he used the word "auctioning off" slaves to the highest bidder. Again he neglected to mention that children were ripped away from their parents and husbands were ripped away from their wives. He failed to mention that the "commodities" were subjected to humiliating inspections where their mouths, ears and genitals were exposed and explored. He failed to mention how some women and men were forced to stand naked in front of groups of people so that "people could get a good look at them." The many rapes that the women commodities suffered were never addressed or alluded to. None of these atrocities were ever mentioned. Only the kindness and benevolence of White slave owners were discussed. Only the White slave owners' willingness to clothe, feed, and house their slaves was examined in detail.

My seventh grade history teacher also stressed how Whites "shared" their religions, customs, and culture with their slaves. He explained how some masters taught their slaves how to read, allowed them to attend church, gave them time off on holidays, and other acts of kindness. Again there was no mention of forced sex on women, painful beatings, mutilation, branding, poor food, or anything else negative. Only the perspective that demonstrated the generosity and humanity of good old White Americans were discussed in his classroom.

Needless to say, attending my history class was emotionally draining. It left me angry, insulted, and most of all, powerless. Many times I would leave class exhausted from fighting with myself. While my teacher shared his warped perspective of slavery, I debated with myself whether to challenge him. I would plead with my inner self to say something to set the record straight. I desperately wanted to speak up for myself and for all Black people, but I didn't have the guts to. Fear prevented me from raising my hand, questioning my teacher's views, and participating in class. Fear of retribution prevented me from sticking up for my race.

Since I acted like a coward, I felt embarrassed by my actions. I couldn' believe that I was same person that attempted to drown a girl in a toile commode. I couldn't believe that I was the same person that could challeng teachers about Black saints. I couldn't believe that I was the same persor that argued and fought so viciously with my siblings. Now I saw mysel as a wimp, a scaredy-cat, a punk, and other words that were reserved fo people who had little backbone. I felt ashamed to be SharRon, and I slowly started hating myself.

Too embarrassed to share my cowardice with my friends, I slowly began to withdrew from Black people. I didn't feel worthy of their friendship since I didn't have the gumption to speak up for us. God knows how much I prayed to have just a little bit of Dr. King's or Malcolm's strength to address my teacher's lies. But I didn't. I was a defeated and deflated Black girl with no allies to defend the Black race. My eight-year battle with school prejudice had emotionally drained me. My resolve was failing, and my emotional resilience was deteriorating. I was sinking.

To my chagrin, the Oreo kid made no attempt to develop a friendship with me or other Blacks even after hearing the degrading remarks in history class. I am not even sure if the comments affected him because he continued to laugh in class and associate with the White students, who felt that slavery was a necessary and charitable thing to do to uncivilized Africans. He never showed any hostility or animosity whatsoever, which made me hate him more. What a fool! How could he hate himself so much?

Unfortunately, I sometimes still witness Black professionals laughing at degrading remarks about Blacks and other minorities to gain acceptance. I still see Blacks accept mistreatment or second-class treatment to be with the "in" group. I still see Blacks, who are ignorant about slavery, willing to accept and embrace the opinions of White authors without investigating and researching history for themselves. I still hate it, but as I matured, I now understand it. When you don't have the power to speak up or if you don't have alliances to offer protection from retribution, it is too risky to go into battle alone; so you try to go along to get along. You sacrifice a little of yourself and your soul. I am not proud of it, but I have been guilty of "playing the game" to fit in. However, I was not too successful at it because I was so emotionally wounded that concealing my pain was impossible. Thankfully, when I graduated from college, I had great mentors who taught me ways to address racist comments diplomatically, emphatically, and politically. To all of my mentors, thank you!

When the school year was almost over, one White female teacher mustered up enough courage to challenge the teaching methods of the racist history teacher. I am not sure how effective her attempts were because she was new to the school district and had no allies. The school system was tightly controlled by well-connected White men, so I am sure that her concerns fell on deaf ears. As an adult, I now understand that her actions were courageous yet precarious. She jeopardized her job and reputation to challenge injustice. Despite being White, I am convinced that being young and female prevented her from being heard and respected by the good old boys who ran the school system. Yet she took a risk and stood on the side of justice. At that point in my life, I needed to see that people like her existed. I needed to witness and hear of teachers sacrificing for me because I felt that I had already sacrificed enough of my spirit just to survive.

My last year at the middle school was a breaking point, but also a blessing. I was hurt and felt dehumanized by an insensitive teacher and an uncaring school system. However, I swore to myself that I would not allow fear to prevent me from speaking up and out. I may not have power or resources to challenge a situation directly, but I do have the power to unite with others to affect change. I also decided that my spiritual health was too important to be a party in my own oppression. I hated myself for too long for not speaking up, and I would rather speak up and be proud of myself than to feel like a shameful coward. I am no longer paralyzed by fear because I can depend on me, just God and me.

## CHAPTER 9

# Let me *In*

ON THE LAST day of school, I walked home instead of riding the school bus back to my part of town, Chocolate City. I did not feel like listening to people playing the Dozens, and I didn't want to be the target of any more jokes. I was tired, bone tired. Throughout the entire school year, I had endured mean-spirited comments from both races. And on the bus home, I endured hurtful comments from people who I desperately wanted to embrace me. But for some reason, they did not like me or welcome me. And so, I walked and I thought. I tried to make sense of it all. What was I doing or not doing? How could I get into the "in" groups? I did not mind the White kids disliking me, but I wanted to understand how could I make the Black kids like and accept me? Why didn't I belong? I walked slowly as I tried to make sense of my outsider status.

During my walk home, I analyzed the failed strategies I used to gain acceptance into the "in" crowd. Since I was going to junior high school in the fall, I needed to find a way to make new friends or just make fewer enemies. When we moved to Sikeston, I initially tried to be helpful to make friends. I helped with chores, did homework, and helped friends sell cupcakes for money; but that didn't work. I laughed at jokes that were not funny and tried to use the most current colloquialisms, but I was not too good at that either. I tried to be sexy like the other girls and snuck makeup to wear during school. That strategy ended when I forgot to wash the makeup off before I got home. Getting the beat down from my mother deterred me from trying that again. But what worked somewhat was buying people doughnuts, some would called it bribery, but I called it developing friendships.

Every morning, I would buy a few Black girls doughnuts and try to interact with them before school started. When I did not provide doughnuts, I was not allowed to associate with them. So I understood that doughnuts were my admission price into the cool crowd. I am embarrassed to admit that I bought doughnuts for months just to be allowed to rub elbows with the girls who existed on the periphery of that group. I was excluded from the middle school movers and shakers. I didn't have my own money, so I stole money from my mother's purse just to ensure that I had my entry fee into the world of popularity—the coveted doughnuts. Even though our family was financially struggling, my need for acceptance into the in crowds overruled my concern for me and siblings. I wanted in! And if doughnuts provided the ticket, I bought doughnuts.

The girls must have sensed my desperation to be their friends because they ordered me around like a puppy dog. They made demands like "Go get my books," "Go get me extra milk," "Give me your fries," "Give me your cookies," "Do my homework," and "Take this to my locker." Whatever they told me to do, I did. When they wanted my lunch, I gave it even if it meant being hungry for the rest of the day. When they wanted to wear my coat, I let them even if it meant me being cold. When they wanted me to do their homework, I did it even if it meant that I had stay up late to do mine. I was being manipulated, but I did not know it. To me, I was just being part of the group. But to others, who were only too willing to tell me, I was being punked. They eagerly informed me that I was being played and that I was being a fool. In some ways, I knew that I was being laughed at, but my hunger for acceptance was greater than my need for respect. I was desperate! I was in dire need of validation, so whatever I needed to be and almost whatever I needed to do to confirm my worth and my visibility, I did. I know it sounds pathetic, but it was true.

After about three months of feeling like a flunky and working harder than a slave, I stopped. I did not give any warning or any explanations. The guilt of taking money from my mother's purse was gnawing away at my spirit. And I finally started to feel like a fool. Something clicked in my spirit, and I finally accepted that I was being taken advantage of. I knew people were laughing at me for months, but for some reason, the ridicule finally hurt me deep enough for me to stop. I finally felt humiliated enough to make a change. I just ended that dog-and-pony show and refused to do any more favors and to comply with any more orders. I made a decision—no more doughnuts, no more errands, no more kissing up, no more homework assignments, no more sharing my lunch, no more anything. I spent my time in the library away from unwelcoming Black and White students. Privately

I nursed my emotional wounds caused by my own self-orchestrated public humiliation and self-choreographed degradation.

I thought about my conciliatory behavior during my walk home. What made me sell my soul to be accepted? Why would I be willing to risk not only myself but my family? Why would I succumb to stealing to be a groupie? I asked myself some hard questions, but I had no answers. The only answer that resonated within me was that I wanted *friends*! I wanted to see what it felt like to be *in*. I had existed on the fringes and survived in the periphery for so long that I hungered for acceptance, acknowledgement, and approval. I wanted to be and to feel a part of a family and a community. Our family moved so much that we did not have familial ties or established roots. We were always in transition and always in crisis. I knew that my time in any community was limited, so I felt that I needed to devise ways to develop friendships quickly. I wanted to feel connected. So in essence, I bought friends. I bought friends with my time, talent, and money; but I never felt treasured. I never fully felt liked or respected. I barely felt tolerated, but for some reason that was enough for me.

Unfortunately, my demeaning, yet totally unconscious, strategy of buying friends started again every time we moved. It became my way of coping with constant relocation. It was how I dealt with the fear of meeting new people, and the anticipation of rejection. It was how I handled the process of proving myself worthy of their companionship. I did not see my destructive pattern. If I did, I would have stopped it. All I knew was that I did not feel like I was enough, so I became a chameleon. I became a giver and provider even if it meant that I had to give what I did not have emotionally, spiritually, intellectually, physically, and financially. I felt that I had to earn friendships and earn love. I had to perform and exceed expectations just to be included and accepted. I had to do/ be something or give something if I wanted to be welcomed and embraced.

It took a long time for me to accept that I was selling myself short. In some ways, I saw my self-degrading behavior. And even when I did not want to mentally acknowledge that I was behaving in ways that did not support me, my body knew. My body rebelled with crushing bouts of anxiety, insomnia, and despair. Despite my body's warning signals, I continued to conduct myself in self-debasing ways. I tried to convince myself and to pretend that I did not engage in self-dishonoring ways. I rationalized my behavior. I told myself that I was just being a wonderful friend, caring girlfriend, and a generous lover. But the truth was that I had low esteem and, I was scared of being left out, that I did not feel as if I was worthy enough of being liked and loved for being me, SharRon. Years of bad experiences in schools had validated my feelings of worthlessness and infected me with the *disease to please*.

The walk home was long. Sometimes, I would just stop and sit down on the curb because my thoughts weighed me down. I really wanted to hide when I not only recognized but accepted that some of the rumors about me being a kiss ass were true. I felt embarrassed and humiliated by my actions, and my spirit was filled with regret. I rehearsed "woulda, shoulda, and coulda" scenarios as if I would have an opportunity to redo those experiences. I wanted and needed a do-over so that I could repair my shattered image and rebuild my self-esteem, but I knew that was impossible. Shame and disappointment overwhelmed me as I relived and replayed my obsequious behavior. I needed to forgive myself, but I did not know how. Who was I? I did not know anymore. All I knew was that I did not want to be who and what I had been. That was the only thought that came out of my one-hour walk home.

I finally got home to our small house in Chocolate City. The walk was tiring, and the thinking was hard. I had much to think about this summer. Junior high was going to be different, it had to be. However, I was not sure what different meant. But whatever happened, I knew that I could depend on God, but I was not sure if God could depend on me.

## CHAPTER 10

# Living in a Hostile Environment

TWO DAYS AFTER my long walk home and my resolve to be different in junior high school, my father informed us that we were moving again. This time we were moving to Jefferson City (JC), Missouri, where he accepted the position as school chaplain for Lincoln University. Without much emotion or regrets, our family once again packed our belongings, said good-bye to our friends, forwarded our mail, and off we went to JC. Unlike the other moves, this relocation was a welcome change because I wanted to flee the painful memories of Sikeston Middle School. I wanted to have an opportunity to recreate myself, to have a new start. I had high hopes that JC and Lincoln University would be a new beginning for me. That it would be an opportunity to redeem myself in some ways.

On our trip up to JC, my father explained that Lincoln University was a historically Black university that was founded to educate newly freed Black slaves. I was immediately impressed with Lincoln's legacy and I vowed to take advantage of every resource that the university offered. I hoped that Lincoln would finally provide what I needed to feel important and proud of Black Americans—information about Black people, their inventions, contributions, and events.

When we arrived in JC, we moved into our home in an integrated part of town. Again, back then, integrated meant more White than anything else. We weren't sure if our neighbors were nice or mean because they never really acknowledged our presence. When we first moved to the neighborhood, we spoke to all our neighbors and tried to introduce ourselves to their children. They were always cordial to us, but it always appeared that they were uncomfortable living so close to us. Even though I grew accustomed to this type of behavior, I expected that our neighbors would be more inviting and liberal since most of them taught at the university with my father. Their behavior was so puzzling to me because I couldn't understand how people who taught and worked with Blacks and at a historically Black university could still be uncomfortable living next to Blacks. I would later come to understand that many of the White faculty members resented my family living so close to the other professors' families because we were of a "negative element." Nobody, of course, could or would explain what a "negative element" meant, but I knew it meant Black.

Since the neighborhood children refused our invitation to jump rope and talk, my sister and I decided to use the summer to read books about Black people written by Black authors. We would rise early, finish our chores, and walk two miles to the university campus to check out books about Blacks and study maps about Africa. Unfortunately, on our walks to the university, we would encounter rude remarks from passersby. Since we were physically developing into pretty young ladies, we grew accustomed to hearing disgusting comments about our bodies and beauty. However, we were caught completely off guard when we received crude comments from White teenagers and grown men. We frequently endured comments like "nigger bitch go back to Africa," "monkey bitch," "nigger wench," and other derogatory names. Even though the names made our flesh crawl, we tried our best to hold our heads up high. We even tried to pretend that we didn't hear them, but I am sure it was obvious to them that we heard them loud and clear because we would walk faster when they yelled. We didn't try to walk faster consciously; but when you are scared and your adrenaline is pumping, your body overrules your mind, and your feet move quickly. In the back of our minds, I think we knew we had to walk faster to reach our destination and for our safety.

I remember one incident in particular when we were walking home with our arms loaded with books. A truck full of White teenagers kept passing by us, yelling disgusting names and comments. I wanted to yell back to show them that I wasn't scared of them, but my sister begged me to stay quiet and not provoke them to other actions. She said, "Girl, name calling is harmless, but getting your ass kicked by a truck full of White kids is crazy." I reluctantly agreed with her even though I felt ashamed of myself again. I hated not being able to stand up for myself or my sister. Again I felt powerless and defeated. I must have felt like the slaves felt when their masters degraded them, and they were unable to respond. But it was 1978! Things were supposed to be different. Whites were not supposed to hate Blacks and vice versa. Even though I knew that racial harmony was just an ideal, I hated being reminded of my second-class existence and my powerlessness on a daily basis.

After two months in Jefferson City, our family decided to move again. The entire family was overjoyed because nobody was happy. My father experienced racism at the university and felt alienated from the other teaching staff. Many of the White professors and staff did not interact with some of the Black faculty. I could not understand that. If you are teaching at a historically Black university and are uncomfortable interacting with Blacks, why are you there? If you feel that Blacks are second-class citizens, why teach them? I would later understand that many of the Whites held leadership positions, and felt that teaching Blacks was okay as long as none of the Blacks aspired to leadership, also known as White positions. Some Whites also held paternalistic and condescending views of Blacks. It was as if they were saying, "I don't mind teaching the 'darkies,' I just don't want to live or exist by them." The whole separate but equal mentality was evident to many of the Black teachers and staff, but none felt safe enough to challenge the racist mindsets. Challenging meant fewer opportunities, loss of promotions, and loss of employment. So nobody talked to the administration. The Black staff just talked amongst themselves in attempt to reconcile their conflicted spirits and to assuage their emotionally battered souls.

Life for my mother wasn't much better. My mother had experienced overt racism from obnoxious patients and from a racist supervisor who consistently assigned her menial jobs despite her credentials and experience as a licensed practical nurse. My sister and I endured sexist and racist taunts from rowdy White teenagers and men. My brother had been chased by White kids in the neighborhood, so he was scared to ride his bike. We were all emotionally weary, and so we really didn't mind packing this time. We were moving to Phoenix, Arizona—a place we all hoped would be friendlier. So to us, it was good-bye and good riddance to Jefferson City.

The most important lesson I learned in JC was that I can depend on me for love and appreciation even though others may feel that I am not worth acknowledging. I am important, and I don't need others recognizing my existence to validate my existence. I can stand alone and be complete. However, I did learn the true meaning of fear when the teenagers taunted me, and I felt unable to effectively defend myself physically and emotionally. From that day on, I realized that I needed to develop better coping skills to stand as fearlessly as possible in the face of adversity. I knew I had God; I just hoped that God had me.

## CHAPTER 11

# Traumatic Transitions

OUR DRIVE TO Phoenix was a turning point in my life. Our green Chevy was packed with three growing kids in the back, two adults in the front, and a fidgety toddler in middle. Clothes, blankets, and food were piled under and between us. Despite the discomfort in the crowded space, there was stillness. There were times when we would go hours without talking, as if we all were trying to make sense of the multiple moves and the traumatic transitions that we all endured. I sensed that all of us were broken in some way. We were all hurting, yet unable to explain our pain or unwilling to share our despair. My parents were somewhat estranged from their families, and they had struggled financially, emotionally, and mentally to care and provide for us despite being children themselves. They wore their struggles on their faces and in their spirits. There was heaviness in the car, an uneasiness that engulfed us. So as we traveled down the highway, I traveled down memory lane trying to make sense of the last seven years. What happened and why? I did not have any answers, but I had to find some. I had to process, explore, and examine my experiences. I knew that they were all traumatic; my body showed that. I had gained over thirty pounds, my hair was coming out, my GI system was rebelling, my mind would not rest, and my spirit was sinking. I needed help.

I tried to be still and did my best to recount what I learned in school. Of course, I learned reading, writing, and arithmetic. But I also learned fear, sadness, pain, chaos, isolation, alienation, lack of support, racism, sexism, bigotry, powerlessness, and failure. But most of all, I was confused. I had witnessed Whites being mean to Whites and Blacks being mean to Blacks. I had experienced Whites coming to my rescue, and Whites helping my parents fight racism. But on the other hand, I had witnessed Whites being extremely disresctpful to me, my parents, and grandparents. I had experienced Blacks affirming me and some Blacks despising me. I had experienced the isolation and sadness of being a special-needs student without teachers who cared. I had experienced jealously and hatred from both races, yet had seen both races embrace another race. I had witnessed teachers speak negatively of Native Americans and Africans, but witnessed other teachers celebrate and honor diversity. All of these experiences left me confused. There was no consistency; no rules to help me navigate living in the world as a Black girl. I wondered what all of the differences meant, but I had no one to speak with or speak to. And so, I sat looking out the window as if answers would appear in the trees, on the ground, or in the sky.

As I looked out the window, tears fell from my eyes and watered my shirt. Even though the tears were huge and came for hours, the water from my eyes paled in comparison to the bleeding in my heart. I cried because I was emotionally tired. I was tired of being strong and pretending like I was strong. I cried because it was expected that I deal with adult problems with only childhood experiences and juvenile understanding. I cried because the constant relocations made me feel unbalanced and unstable. I cried because I felt hopeless and helpless. I cried because there was no other way to cleanse myself from my feelings of pain, frustration, and despondency. I cried in the car because I did not have the freedom to cry in school without being judged, taunted, or ridiculed. I did not have the freedom to cry at home without being reminded that my life was better than my parents' life. I was always reminded that I should feel happy that I had the opportunity to attend "great," but to me racist, schools. I cried to release the despair of my unpredictable and painful life. My heart was aching, and my body was raw with emotion. Despite the endless tears, my parents never said a word. They had their own issues and their own fears which created an ominous ambience in the car.

The trip to our new life in Arizona was long. The drives in the dark were sometimes unbearable. I had dreams, disturbing dreams. I had dreams that validated the powerlessness that I felt for me and my family. I dreamed of being attacked and being seriously injured. I dreamed of the KKK (Ku Klux Klan) torturing me and my parents. I dreamt of us being homeless, begging for food. I dreamed of death. I had dreams that a young girl should never dream. And so, I prayed to God to help me. I prayed to my Black God to protect me. I prayed to God to take away the sadness. I prayed for stability. I prayed for safety. I prayed for an adult to listen to me, and on a few occasions, I prayed to die. I prayed!

I am not sure if my prayers will be answered or if the tides will turn. I got to wait until we get to Phoenix to see. But through it all, I know that I can depend on me, just God and me.

## CHAPTER 12

# God and Me

*HI GOD! I know you are there. I am tired of sitting in the back seat and I am tired of sitting in this car. How far is Arizona anyway? The car is hot, and the hot air from the windows is drying out my mouth. It is too hot. Mommy and Daddy keep arguing, and Patrick keeps lying on me. I want to pop him in his head, but I know that I would get in trouble if I hit him. I am tired of moving too, and Daddy never helps us pack. He only packs his office, and we got to pack everything else. I want to tell him, "Since you keep making us move, you pack everything." But I don't want to get a whooping or get slapped. I know Momma probably already told him that anyway because she is tired of moving too. How did I get two tired parents? Why are we always broke? Why don't the White people like us? Why am I getting so fat? I know you hold the whole world in your hands, so please help me. This seems unfair. I know you are working everything out, but please hurry up. I am not sure how much longer I can hold on. Thank you and I love you!*

I am always asked how I knew God was present in the midst of my pain. And, honestly, I cannot answer that. Just like I don't remember not being able to walk or talk, I don't remember not knowing about God. I just knew because my family always talked about God and prayed to God. When we were not talking about God, we were at church singing and learning about God. And if we were not learning about God at church, we were arguing and debating about God and biblical principles with family members. There was never an opportunity to not know God. God and God conversations were just like breathing to me. I just knew that God was there, and I did not question it. The Ghanaians believe that "No one has to teach a child that God exists. God just is." I share that belief.

My earliest understanding of the power of God in my life was watching people in my grandfather's church, my aunt's church, and my father's church during devotional service. I heard people share challenging problems, horrific experiences, and sad stories. But after every story, I also heard how God brought people through or brought people out; we called these testimonies. Even though I did not fully understand all of the testimonies or how God operated, I accepted that God existed. It was part of my upbringing and my socialization. And even though I sometimes did not feel that God cared about me, I had an understanding that God was there giving me strength, power, and determination. I felt that God was empowering me when I felt paralyzed by fear and frightened by my feelings of being invisible. I knew God even though I could not articulate how I knew. And since my parents were not capable of providing the parental direction and support that I needed, I had no other choice but to embrace God. God was my parent, my confidant, my protector, my teacher, my friend, my supporter. I knew that I could depend on God!

I experienced God differently as an adult. God is no longer a man to me; God has no gender. God is no longer confined to church; God resides in me. God is not only helpful; God is my help. God is always available. God does not detach from me when I behave in ways that are less than stellar. I don't have a dichotomous relationship with God either. God is with me in times of my success and in my times of shame. God is with me in my times of celebration and in my times of chaos. God is with me in times of great humiliation and in times of great honor. God is with me when I do well, and God is with me when I do poorly. God is always there!

Imani Evans, an amazing therapist and friend, says that God is *the* Source and people are resources. As a result, I now understand that I can depend on me mainly because God, the Source, has prepared people (resources) to serve as vessels, conduits, and mentors for and with me. It is my responsibility to identify the resources that have been provided and use them to develop emotionally, physically, spiritually, socially, intellectually, and mentally. My dependence on God does not excuse or exempt me from taking action needed to live life abundantly. My dependence on God empowers me to act. My dependence on God demands that I *do* and *be* because God's presence endows me, fortifies me, sustains me, and directs me. I can depend on me because God is with me, in me, around me, in front me, and behind me. I am surrounded and protected by God's presence.

My most important adult revelation is that everybody has their own way of understanding God. God may be a still quiet voice, may manifest a intuition, may feel like a spiritual urging, may be experienced as energy or/and show up in various forms of worship. Whatever the method, mode, experience or process, God is always available and accessible.

*Daddy said that we should be in Phoenix in about three hours. Get ready God! I know that I will need you again. Whatever I face, I know that I can depend on You and me, mostly You and just a little of me. But that's all I need, right?*

# EPILOGUE

IT HAS BEEN over thirty years, and I still feel remnants of my childhood experiences. Thankfully, the memories which were hurtful are now healed. The recollections that were once a source of pain are now a great source of help and hope to me and to others. Every day, as I travel through life, I am reminded that my childhood journey only slowed and stifled me, but it did not stop me. I learned the meaning of perseverance; and most of all, I learned that I could depend on me, just God and me.

During my journey to wholeness and health, I realized that the "adult" me was sometimes controlled by the "child" me. The child me who was scared to use her voice, who tried too hard to fit in, who was socially awkward, who accepted disrespectful behavior from friends and family, who would not ask for help, who was angry at the world, who used food and distraction to numb pain, and who struggled with low self-esteem was limiting my adult life. My journey revealed that not only was healing necessary, but actively participating in my healing was critical. I am grateful now that the fearful little girl in me rarely surfaces; and when she does, I remind her that she is powerful, intelligent, confident, resourceful, beautiful, and delightful. I remind her that she is a child of God in whom God is well pleased.

I also learned that the healing process is extremely variable, and the journey may involve multiple attempts and multiple processes. Successful healing is never a straight line or a single event. The truth is, healing is hard and requires work: work to get started and work to stay committed.

The first and most important part of my healing journey, my work, was to fully identify my pain. I had to "name" the pain—what was it, what caused it, and what did I do to survive it. So on my healing journey, I identified that my pain was called fear, loneliness, inadequacy, uncert[illegible] and invisibility. I was able to recognize how my childhood and c[illegible] experiences wounded me. And most importantly, I was able to [illegible]

I coped. Identifying my coping behaviors allowed me to see destructive patterns that continuously robbed me of my self-worth, self-respect, self-esteem, and progress.

With the help of countless others, I also realized that my coping behaviors were also extreme. My coping mechanisms were either black or white, there was no middle ground and no balance. For example, I sometimes coped with fear by avoidance, denial, and detours. At other times, I addressed fear by aggressively confronting it. I sometimes coped with feelings of inadequacy by refusing to participate in events and by refusing to interact with people who I felt were more accomplished and confident. But at other times, I coped with my feelings of inadequacy by putting excessive pressure on myself to achieve. But after every achievement, I felt empty. Winning and exceeding everyone's expectations did not assuage my feelings of insufficiency and deficiency. It took me years to realize that outward success could not compensate for or correct my internal feelings of worthlessness.

I coped with loneliness by becoming more reclusive and not making friends; I isolated myself. And when I mustered enough courage to interact, I made the wrong friends and interacted with the wrong family members. I allowed, and sometimes actively participated in, the disrespect that I received. It is sad to say, but sometimes I even unconsciously and indirectly orchestrated and choreographed my own continued abuse and mistreatment. My childhood experiences made exploitation, manipulation, neglect, and mistreatment feel normal. And I had no other barometer to assess what healthy and loving behavior "looked like." So I spent many of my adult years learning what "normal" supportive treatment was, and after I learned it, I never accepted anything less. Learning was not easy; it required me to be analytical, honest, vulnerable, and intentional. I had new standards, new expectations, and new requirements for myself and others. I sometimes even had to insist that the new expectations and requirements be honored. I lost friends and love ones, but I found *me*!

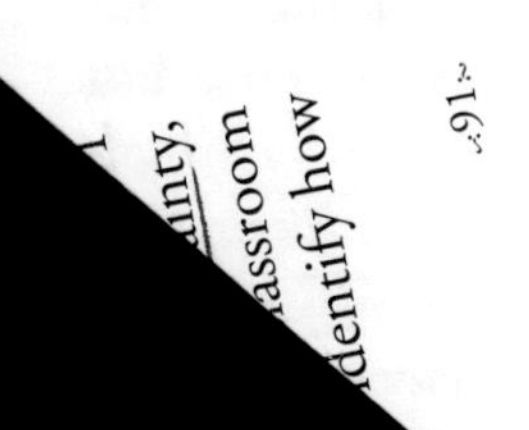

ı, I started to reconstruct my life to better support
ıade myself a priority by protecting my physical,
l health. I released negative people from my life and
ıg people into my inner circle. I started celebrating
oring my voice, which fostered my self-esteem.
strength that carried me through eight years o

instructional hell. I looked in the mirror and realized that I was visible, present, and amazing.

I also realized that my childhood equipped me in ways that I could never imagine. It equipped me to deal with uncertainty, transitions, ridicule, being left out, physical pain, emotional pain, not being recognized, and not being included. My pastor, Dr. Kenneth Samuel, says that sometimes affliction teaches the best lessons in life. So I realized that my childhood hardships prepared me to successfully deal with challenges, adversity, and pitfalls; they provided me with a resilience and wisdom that few others share. And as I now navigate and function in the world, I realize that I am ready, willing, and prepared to challenge, change, conquer, and confront. I am not scared of being alone. I am not frightened to challenge the status quo. I am not fearful of failure. I am not afraid of success. I am not discouraged by hard work. I am not reluctant to try something new. I am not concerned about being acknowledged. I am okay with being different. I am here and God is with me.

I wish that I could say that all of the healing and growth occurred overnight, but I can't. It took many years to change my mindset, correct my maladaptive behaviors, restructure my life, and to change my responses to real and/or perceived injustices, prejudices, and inequalities. It was difficult yet doable. It was a journey, a journey that I successfully made and continue to make. So yes, I can depend on me! And yes, you can depend on you.

What I learned on my journey is that healing is attainable. I learned that emotional and spiritual healing requires five important steps:

1) **Embrace your experiences and extract the lessons learned along the way.**

Healing demands that experiences are examined, explored, analyzed, and acknowledged. Why? You can not address what you will not admit. And in our experiences lie valuable insight, powerful messages, needed instructions, significant discoveries as well as helpful warnings. Our experiences educate and introduce us to who we really are. Life is a classroom and our experiences are the curricula. For my healing, I had to own the hurt, in order to get help and restore my hope. I had to embrace, and accept, my life experiences. I had to extract, *remove*, and *unearth* the learnings. There is an African proverb that states, "No one is without knowledge except those who asks no questions." Ask yourself the hard questions and your truth will be revealed.

2) **Enlist the support of others to champion you and to travel with you on your healing journey.**

Isolation can be deadly, especially in the face of challenges and adversity. Suffering alone only serves to exacerbate feelings of despair, desperation, and depression. And enduring sorrow, agony, and other intense emotions and experiences without support, comfort, and encouragement can unnecessarily delay your healing journey. If I had known then what I know now, I would have allowed and invited people to travel with me on my healing process. I would have used their words of wisdom to rebuild and revive my shattered self-esteem. I would have used their hugs and kisses to soothe my wounded soul. I would have used their accolades and affirmations to restore my self-image and my self-identify. I would have used their positive declarations to help me remember my self-worth. I would have used their admonitions to improve my critical thinking skills. If I would have enlisted the support of others, my journey could have easier and my load lighter. If I had trusted the process, I would not have tried to hide my shame, pain, and embarrassment. I would have been more authentic, vulnerable, and honest with myself and them. More importantly, my journey would have been shorter, more successful, and less stressful. Enlist, *recruit* people who have demonstrated that they are people of integrity, who have successfully overcome experiences similar to yours, who have conquered habits/temptations similar to yours, who are open to love and be loved, and are willing to take the healing journey with you. The African proverb informs us that "A person is a person because of other persons." Accept your persons into your process and be blessed. You are worth it and you deserve it.

3) **Erase negativity from your life, and replace pessimism and toxic people with affirming people and experiences.**

Negativity and pessimism rob you of your spiritual power. They are energy drainers. They drain your joy, peace, hope, and patience. Negativ people are energy leeches that have the potential to suck the life out of all. Unfortunately, some of the most negative people in our lives are people who are the closest to us, people who have known us for a long time, and people who are not supportive of our growth/change. Some people sabotage your journey to wellness by erecting roadblocks to discourage you. Some attempt to delay your journey by being distractors or causing distractions for you. Others are bolder and create detours and diversions that threaten to disrupt and derail you. Erase, *remove* them immediately. If people are not supporting, encouraging, and affirming you, they are hindering or hampering you. If you don't want to remove them completely, transition them from confidant to colleague, friend to associate, and family to casual acquaintance. Only people who are vital and are willing to play a significant and supportive role in your healing process deserve to be close and to have continued access to you. Healing requires that you confront yourself spiritually, emotionally, physically, mentally, intellectually, and socially. Remind yourself that you desire and deserve only people who are committed to your healing in your life; energy drainers are not welcome.

4) **Embark on your new life and be committed to your continued healing, and to assisting in the healing of others.**

The hardest part and the most important part of healing is making the decision to heal. The statement seems so simple, but the process is not easy. Healing is not always fun; healing hurts. Healing requires determination and tenacity. It requires challenging yourself, correcting yourself, and communicating with yourself. Healing also demands that you celebrate yourself and honor yourself. Healing is not a destination; it is a journey, an intentional journey. It requires patience, and the African proverb reminds us that "At the bottom of patience there is heaven." Your healing will give you an opportunity to experience heaven on earth. Go for it! Move! Get started! Then remember to reach back and help heal others. I am convinced that God blesses people to be a blessing to others. Every time I share my story, facilitate workshops, preach/teach, and counsel people, I am reminded of my own progress and growth. Just the small reminders solidify my commitment to my own journey and confirms my faith in the power of healing.

5) **Expect that God's provision and protection ARE always present; you are never alone.**

In the Christian faith, we are taught that God is a near and present help. I know that other faith traditions have similar beliefs. Anticipate that God is present! God is love! God is power! God is light! God is yours! You are never alone. The Nigerian proverb affirms that "God will help you if you get up." So get up, and then look up! God is present in you and around you. Be encouraged because you don't have to walk your healing journey by alone.

I invite you to reflect on the five steps listed above. The steps helped me, and I pray that the steps are instrumental in your own healing. Take your time and go deep within your spirit. Be honest with yourself even if the honesty hurts. Your answers are already there for you and in you. The coaching journal provided will hopefully point you in the right direction and guide you on your healing journey.

I thank God for my journey, and I have learned a few valuable lessons along the way. I have learned that blessings are often times in the breaks. Help is often times in the hurt. Success is often times in the suffering. Clarity is often times in the chaos. Triumphs are often time in tribulations. Strength is often exposed in struggle. Love is often times realized in loss. Faith is often seen in failure. Deliverance is sometimes part of despair. Passion is often seen in purpose. And most of all, greatness is always found in God!

I wish you success on your healing journey. I pray that you affirm that you have what it takes to be your best self. I pray that you affirm that you are a blessing to yourself and others. I pray that you affirm that your past will never dictate your future. I pray that you look in the mirror and say to yourself daily that "I Can Depend on Me, Just God and Me"

Blessings!

# ACKNOWLEDGMENTS

MY GREATEST THANKS goes to God, the ultimate Creator, Healer, and Sustainer. Thank you, God, for helping me believe in me and for surrounding me with people who loved me when I did not fully love myself.

I am grateful to my son, Tariq Reche Jamison Abdul-Haqq. You are one of the best presents that God has given me. I am grateful and honored to be your mom and mentor. I did not understand the value of loving another human being until I experienced the impact and power of my love on you. You were an incredible teacher to me.

I am grateful to Reche Tariq Abdul-Haqq. You are not only my son's father, but you were the first person who believed in me and encouraged me to write *I Can Depend on Me*. You read, you edited, and you encouraged. I am grateful.

I am grateful to Jackie Dyer Carr. You have been my friend for over twenty-five years. You never let distance, depression, difference, divorce, or disease divide us. You are my most treasured friend. Thank you!

I am grateful for my sister-friend, Bonita McAllister. You always challenged me to honor myself and showed me ways to do it in a way that lifted my spirits and my confirmed self-worth. Thank you!

I am grateful for Sonia Ventura. When depression prevented me from taking care of my son, you stepped in and provided the guidance he required and the encouragement that I needed. You lost friends due to your commitment to me and my son. I can never repay you for your sacrifice.

I am grateful for Valeria Lynn Gibson. Thanks so much for taking care of the details so that I could go after my dreams. I so appreciate you.

I am grateful for Deborah Mance and Steven Butler. Thank God for supporting me in ways that only you can know. Thank You!

I am grateful to Rita Yawn. Your dedication and commitment to me and this project is so appreciated. Your unique perspective was helpful in making sure that my voice was heard.

I am grateful to Kim McNair, who challenged me to be vulnerable even when I wanted to hide the parts of me that I was ashamed of.

I am grateful to Janis Williams and Carrole Moss for reading and editing my book. I so appreciate your time, talent, and commitment to me and to this project.

I am grateful to Imani Evans who continues to be my trusted therapist and friend. Thanks for listening and processing with me.

I am grateful to Momma C, Carrole Moss. Thanks for being a mother to me and a grandmother to my son. You were there during one of the most difficult times in my life, and I thank you. You loved me, supported me, and showed up in ways that I could only hope for. You have blessed my life, and you continue to bless me. I love you Momma C.

I am grateful for Mother Lucille Grinnell. You were the first person at Victory for the World Church, who told me that I was loved. You were the impetus of some very important healing in my life. Thank you and I love you.

I am grateful for my pastor, Dr. Kenneth L. Samuel. Your messages of empowerment, faith, and love were healing salve to my wounded soul. I am honored to serve in the pulpit under your leadership.

I am grateful for Rev. Troy Saunders. Thanks for encouraging me when I was too scared to pray and to preach in public. Your encouragement and belief in me made me believe more in myself.

I am grateful for Dr. Kathi Martin. Thanks for being a good example of women leadership in ministry. I appreciate your help and mentoring. Thank You!

am grateful to the women of Infinity Diamond Club. Thank you for elieving in me and for allowing me to share my gifts with you.

am grateful for my sister, Tiphanie VanDerLugt. You always told me that ou loved me no matter what.

am grateful to my siblings, Chatone Jamison and Patrick Jamison.

am grateful to my parents, Rev. Franklin Jamison III and Dorethia amison. You had the difficult task of raising four very different children vith little money and support. Thank so much for introducing me to God, nd for demanding that God have a prominent role in my life. Thank you o much for introducing me to struggle and modeling resilience. Thanks or trying to protect me even when you had little protection for yourself. I ove you both.

# COACHING GUIDE

***1) Embrace your experiences and extract the lessons learned along the way.***

We all have experiences that have shaped us. Some experiences showed us our strengths. Some experiences exposed our needs for growth. Some experiences confirmed our values. Some experiences broaden our perspectives. Some experiences uncovered parts of us that we did not know existed. Some experiences taught us heartache. Some experiences showed us love. What have your experiences taught you about you? Here are some questions to help you reflect.

1. What experiences have caused you the greatest joy? Why?
2. What experiences have caused you pain?
3. What experiences were the most challenging?
4. What experiences do you still struggle with?
5. What strengths were revealed?
6. What opportunities did the experiences reveal?
7. What areas of growth were identified?
8. What did the experiences reveal about you?
9. How did you honor/celebrate the good experiences?
10. How did you analyze/examine/process the painful experiences?
11. How have you dealt or how are you dealing with the hurt caused by the bad event/experiences?

# Personal Reflections

Pain has a name. The clearer you see it, the more effective you are moving through it. Why? The better the diagnosis, the more effective the treatment. So what is the name of your pain (*i.e.,* fear, failure, lack of self-esteem, etc.)? Let's begin the healing journey together.

1. What is the name of your pain and why? What caused it? Who caused or created it?
2. Where and when does it hurt?
3. When do you have emotional flare-ups?
4. What are you pain triggers?
5. How do you respond to your triggers and flare-ups?
6. Do your responses support and serve you? How?
7. How does you pain manifest in your body now? How did the manifestations change over the years?
8. How do you determine when healing occurs or when you are in the healing process?
9. How do you act out when in painful situations?
10. What has your pain revealed to you?

# Personal Reflections

**2) *Enlist the support of others to champion you and to travel with you on your healing journey.***

One of the hardest lessons that I had to learn was that it was okay to ask for help. It was acceptable to seek assistance. It was useful to have support. It was not vain to have a few cheerleaders in your life. Why? Because success, growth, and healing rarely happen in isolation. Separation and seclusion are detrimental to recovery; exposure and encouragement are vital. You need people, and people need you. Positive connections are critical. So who have you recruited to be on your healing team? Who is your support system? Who have you selected to travel with you on your journey to spiritual, emotional, and physical wellness and wholeness?

1. Who is on your healing team? Name them and their roles?
2. Who is your mentor, therapist, or coach? What is their role in your life?
3. How and when do you coach yourself?
4. Who can tell you the truth? Who can you "hear" truth from?
5. What are some consistent themes that your support system shares with you about you?
6. What shared information surprises you? Confronts you? Concerns you? Affirms you? Celebrates you?
7. What organizations and/or groups are available to address your healing issue/need?
8. How do your track or document your healing journey?
9. Who are your three closest confidants? Why were each person selected?
10. What do you need to share or reveal to support your healing journey?

# Personal Reflections

### *3) Erase negativity from your life, and replace pessimism and toxic people with affirming people and experiences.*

Negative emotions and negative people drain your energy and prevent you from harnessing the power you need to move forward in your healing process. Negative feelings and negative people cause you to doubt yourself and your ability. They create feelings of hopelessness and despair. But you have the power to infuse your life with positive emotions and positive people, so let's reflect how.

1. How do you identify and deal with toxic people in your life?
2. What boundaries and borders have you set to limit negativity?
3. How do you deal with people who sabotage your healing and growing efforts?
4. What makes you susceptible and vulnerable to toxicity and sabotage?
5. What prevents you leaving the toxic personal and family relationships?
6. How do you know when you need to make personnel changes in your life? And when you make changes, how do enforce it so that the change would be honored?
7. How did you know when people are helpful, hopeful, and healing? And if so, how do you support their continued presence in your life?
8. What does affirming mean to you, and how do you determine if a person is affirming you?
9. How do your friends/family celebrate and honor you for who you are and for who you are not?
10. What five qualities do you most value? How do you ensure that those qualities are present in your relationships?

# Personal Reflections

4) ***Embark on your new life and be committed to your continued healing and to assisting in the healing of others.***

I love the word embark because it indicates movement. When you are embarking on a new life, you are getting on board emotionally, physically, spiritually, and intellectually to *move* to a new emotional destination, to a new mindset, and to a new way of being. Embark is an action verb, and action requires that *you* do something. Why? *Nothing in life happens without action*; so move, travel, and progress toward the life that you want! And help as you heal, and heal as you help. By assisting and supporting others in their journey, you will reinforce and fortify the positive changes that you make in your own life. Once you can teach and assist others, you will validate that you have learned and are learning. Ask yourself the following questions to assess how you are moving and progressing on your own journey.

1. Where movements or changes do you need to make in your life? Why?
2. What causes you to procrastinate? Why? How can you address the causes?
3. What steps are the hardest for you to make?
4. Where do you usually get sidetracked? Why? What can you do to limit getting sidetracked?
5. What do you want to achieve? Why?
6. What's your passion? Purpose?
7. What actions are you taking to live out your passion and purpose? What's your strategy?
8. How are you sharing what you have learned with others?
9. What are you learning by supporting and assisting others?
10. What are you learning about yourself?

# Personal Reflections

### 5) *Expect that God's provision and protection are always present; you are never alone.*

Everybody has a "Source" even though we call the Source by many names. I call my Source, God, and you may call your Source something else. During my toughest times and my darkest nights, I knew that God was my provider. God was my provider of strength, power, determination, comfort, and support. I never doubted God's provision even if I could not articulate how I knew. I also knew that God was my protector. Even when I felt insecure and defenseless, God provided safety and security. You may say to yourself that if God was my protector, why did I experience so much pain. I choose to see it differently. Without God acting as a shield, I would have been wounded beyond repair. I would not have had the emotional reserve and fortitude to endure and thrive in a hostile environment. I would not have had the emotional stamina and resilience to persevere. I would not have had the strength to survive and to share my story with you. Your Source is always there too; you are never alone. What is your Source? How can you tap into your Source of healing?

1. What role does daily mediation play in your life?
2. How do you connect with your Source?
3. How do you quiet yourself during trials and adversity?
4. How do you hear the still voice inside of you?
5. What do you do to feel the presence and power of your Source?
6. What makes up your spiritual life? How does your spiritual life serve you? What is lacking in your spiritual life? Why?
7. What organizations share your beliefs, and how can you connect with them?
8. What serves as your moral and spiritual compass? Why?
9. How do you see yourself in relation to your Source?
10. If you felt deeply connected to the Source, what would you know for sure? What would you feel? How would it affect your behavior? What would you do differently? What would you continue to do?

# Personal Reflections

Edwards Brothers Malloy
Thorofare, NJ USA
November 26, 2012